GOD'S LOVE FOR MUSLIMS

Communicating Bible Grace and New Life

GOD'S LOVE
FOR
MUSLIMS

Communicating Bible Grace and New Life

Ibrahim Ag Mohamed

Metropolitan Tabernacle, London

GOD'S LOVE FOR MUSLIMS
Communicating Bible Grace and New Life
© Ibrahim Ag Mohamed, 2015

Published by the Metropolitan Tabernacle
Elephant & Castle
London SE1 6SD
www.metropolitantabernacle.org

ISBN 978 1 899046 63 8

Cover design by Andrew Owen

Printed in the United Kingdom

Contents

Today, almost everyone has an opinion about Islam. The purpose of this book is to provide an accurate outline of the Islamic faith to Christians, and to provide a tool that will help them relate to Muslims and communicate the Gospel with informed understanding.

PART I

THE MUSLIM FAITH

Fast growth and expansion

'The religion before Allah is Islam [submission to his will]...'
(Surah 3.19).[1]

THERE ARE CURRENTLY over one billion Muslims around the globe. Islam now has the second largest number of claimed adherents (Christianity being the first). It is also the fastest growing world religion, not in terms of conversions, but through *biological* growth (due primarily to the practice of polygamy, which is legal in many Muslim lands). Every year thirty million Muslims are born.

Islam has spread from the Middle East across the world, dominating many countries. It is also making significant inroads

---

1   *Surah* means chapter. The Qur'an is divided into 114 chapters, divided also into 6,239 verses or *ayah* which means sign, as in Ayatollah (sign of Allah). The verse numbering may differ slightly between the versions of the Qur'an.

into Western nations, the former Soviet Union (perhaps as many as eighty million Muslims), and parts of China.

The following facts – which may surprise you – about the rapid growth of Islam in this country are not intended to convey disapproval but to inspire the desire for souls and mission. We read in the *Church Around the World* (18, no.1, 1987) that in 1945 there was only one mosque in England. Today there are over 1,000 mosques, and more than two million Muslims (up from 100,000 forty years ago). There are now more Muslims than Roman Catholics. In England, 10,000 churches have closed since 1960. By 2020 another 4,000 churches are expected to close, and it is predicted that 1,700 new mosques will have opened by then, many of which will be located on former church sites. The building that housed the church which sent William Carey (the father of modern missions) to India is now a mosque (*World Christian Magazine,* February 1989).

It is claimed that there are 30,000 white British converts to Islam at the moment, and that this number is increasing daily by three to five converts, most of these being British women who marry Muslim men. Twelve percent and twenty-one percent of the population respectively in London and Birmingham is Muslim.[2] In some European countries it is the hope of Muslims that abandoned and empty churches should be turned into mosques as a matter of course. Muslims regard it as a great success when a church closes and is transformed into a mosque. Sharia courts are increasing in number to please the Muslim population, but also to show disapproval of Western laws, believed to be shaped by Christianity.

According to the *Independent* (1st December 2014), the Islamic prophet's name in its various spellings has become the most popular name for new-born boys in England. At least four different spellings of the name Muhammad were among the most popular American boys' names in 2011, according to the Social Security

2   Office for National Statistics, 2011 Census.

Administration.[3] A recent *Times* front page reported that nearly a tenth of infants and toddlers in Britain are now Muslim. It is claimed that one day there will be more practising Muslims than Christians in the UK.

A desire to prevail over the West and the rest of the world

Islam is blossoming and flourishing in the world. The liberal Western democracies have political and social systems which contain the seed of their own demise. There are more than twenty-four million Muslims in Europe. The rising tide of future Islamic numeric dominance is there for all to see.

- At least sixty-five nations in the world are Islamic, with Indonesia having the largest Muslim population.
- The Middle East is exclusively Islamic, and the break-up of the Soviet Union gave birth to six more Islamic nations (Kazakhstan, Turkmenistan, Uzbekistan, Tajikistan, Kyrgyzstan, and Azerbaijan).
- A new mosque opens every week in the United States. In 1990 there were thirty mosques in the United States. Today there are more than 3,000.
- Africa is called by Muslims the Islamic continent.
- In Australia, there were only 800 Muslims in 1955, but there are more than half a million today.
- In France, there are millions of Muslims (mainly from North Africa) and more than 2,000 mosques. On Fridays some streets are taken over by crowds of worshippers because there is not enough room in the mosques. In 1974, there was only one mosque in France. Nowadays, the 'Great Mosque' in Paris records 600 to 700 conversions to Islam every year.
- In Germany, there are four million Muslims (the majority of

---

3   http://religion.blogs.cnn.com – 14th August 2012.

whom are from Turkey), and 2,000 mosques.

- In Belgium, there are more Muslims than Protestants. Twenty-five percent of births are from Muslim parents.

- In the Netherlands, Islam is becoming one of the most important influences in society. In Rotterdam's main square, there is a mosque with Arabic writing on the outside that reads: 'This used to be a church.'

- Every year approximately half a million Muslims enter Europe by immigration.

A way of life

Islam is unique in many ways. Being known as a Muslim is of great importance. Islam is not just a religion, but a civilisation, a culture and a state, being a way of life encompassing religious, political, social, economic, ideological, educational, military and judicial systems. It is an identity where personal freedom is non-existent. Democracy, free will and freedom of expression are mostly disregarded.

There is no separation between state and religion. This is why many Muslims do not draw a line between the Christian faith and Western culture. They wrongly equate Christianity with Roman Catholicism; and they assume that every white person (from the West) must be a Christian. They look at the West and see a society that is marked by freedom to indulge in moral depravity and unbelief; a society in which clergy and political leaders are morally corrupt. They do not recognise their own shortcomings and internal splits, but see only the divisions in Christianity and the undeniable decadence of Western society.

One ideological goal

'Fight against them until idolatry is no more and Allah's religion reigns supreme...' *(Surah 2.193).*

Islam is the only world religion founded since the beginning of the Christian church, and Muslims believe that they are a superior people, the best people ever raised up for mankind *(Surah 3.110; 5.56)*, having been given a superior religion. In most Islamic nations, Christians are not to be taken as friends *(Surah 5.51)*. They are regarded as second-class citizens, 'infidels', and looked down upon as 'dogs' and 'pigs' (unclean).

Islam's ideological goal is to saturate the world with the Muslim faith, and then to impose a religious global state governed by Sharia (Islamic religious law) and a world caliphate. Muslims are commanded to subjugate every person to Islam. They believe that Islam should prevail over all religions *(Surah 9.33)*. The apparent tolerance and the low profile shown by Islam (in the UK for example) would soon be overtaken by the desire for an Islamic state once majority numbers were attained.

Some sobering facts

- The cities of the seven churches in the book of *Revelation* (Ephesus, Smyrna, Pergamos, Thyatira, Sardis, Philadelphia, and Laodicea) – in modern-day Turkey – are all under Islamic control today. Most of them fell before the birth of Islam to corrupted forms of Christianity.
- Many well-known Bible lands and places are now under Islamic rule.
- Modern Israel (as a political entity) does not feature in any Arab world map.
- Egypt, the motherland of Christian monasticism and a theological centre from the time of Origen to Athanasius, is under Islamic domination.
- North Africa, where all Western theology has its roots, where the Latin Fathers Tertullian, Cyprian and Augustine ministered, has been incorporated into the Islamic world.
- The Roman provinces of Asia Minor, the region of Paul's early missionary journeys and of much of the Patristic (early

Christian) theology, have become provinces of Islam.

• Of the five great cities of the ancient church – Rome, Constantinople, Alexandria, Antioch and Jerusalem – only Rome has remained free from Muslim domination.

Not so united, after all

A reality Muslims may not want to admit is that Islam is divided into various sects that often violently oppose each other. There are more than 150 religious groups or Islamic 'denominations', with two main groups: the Sunnis (90%) and the Shias or Shi'ites (10%). The latter group is found predominantly in Iran, and also in Iraq, Afghanistan, Syria, Pakistan, Lebanon, Bahrain and Yemen. Iran is the only Islamic nation which is officially Shia.

The Sunnis – followers of the *sunna* or 'pathway' – base their faith on the Qur'an, but also on the Traditions or *Hadith*.[4] The *Hadith* were put together more than two hundred years after Muhammad's death.[5] Sunnis recognise four Caliphs or 'successors' (Abu Bakr, Umar, Uthman and Ali) as the only true successors to the prophet of Islam. It was during the caliphate of Uthman (AD 644-656) that one single text of the Qur'an was officially approved and all other versions destroyed by fire to avoid any conflicting texts. So the claim by many Muslims that there has only ever been one text of their holy book is not correct.

The Shias are so called because they belong to the *Shi'at 'Ali* (the party of Ali); *shi'at* means 'sect' or 'split'. They regard Ali (Muhammad's son-in-law and cousin) alone as the legitimate successor and heir of the prophet, together with the twelve imams (or leaders) who lineally descended from him. The Shias are divided into many different sects of varying orthodoxy, including the Druzes, the Isma'ilis, and the Kharijis. The Sufis (found in all the

---

4   The collected and authenticated words and deeds of Muhammad.
5   Islam was founded in the seventh century by Muhammad (AD 570-632).

main streams) represent the more mystical element in Islam.

The two groups, Sunni and Shia, have different and contradictory traditions, and have little respect for one another. Historically, the Sunnis have tended to persecute the Shias; this persecution continues today and can involve extremes of violence.

What does 'Islam' mean? A definition

A general knowledge of the faith and practices of Muslims is so helpful as we seek opportunities to speak to Muslims about the Lord Jesus Christ and the Gospel of redeeming grace.

The word *Islam* (from the Arabic *aslama*) means 'surrender', 'submission', and 'subjection', or 'to yield'. It does not mean 'peace' as is sometimes claimed. Therefore a Muslim is *one who submits* – to Allah (or God), his prophet and the Qur'an. It is about an utter allegiance – no questions asked. 'You have not believed until you say, we have submitted ourselves' *(Surah 49.14; cf. 5.111)*. It is a *master-slave* relationship, not a *Father-son* one. It offers no close relationship between God and man. Man's relation to God is that of a slave *(abd)* to his lord. Man was not created in the image of God, but as his slave. *Abdullah* (slave of Allah) is a very common name in Islamic nations. (Clearly this is very different from the Christian doctrine of adoption.)

Even though Islam arose after both Judaism and Christianity (the Islamic lunar calendar starting on 16th July AD 622 approximately), Muslims maintain that it is the oldest religion, because they believe it started with Adam, the first man (not with Muhammad, who was born in about AD 570). However, *Surah 6.14, 163* says that Muhammad was the first to submit to Allah and become a Muslim. Elsewhere, *Surah 7.143* says that Moses was the first Muslim. It is claimed that Noah, Abraham *(Surah 3.66; 4.125)*, David, Solomon, John the Baptist, the Lord Jesus Christ and His apostles (except Paul, who is accused of corrupting Christ's Gospel) were all Muslims *(Surah 5.111; 6.85-87)*. Unlike in true Christianity, they actually believe that *every* child without exception is *born* a Muslim (wherever in the world).

Muslims believe that their religion is the greatest and the most beautiful, and that God has appointed it to be the only true faith *(Surah 2.112; 4.125)*. Unlike Christianity and Buddhism, Islam has not been named after its founder, providing another reason why its adherents believe that it came from God. They say that the name *Islam* has been expressly given to them by Allah.

WHAT DO MUSLIMS BELIEVE?

ISLAM CLAIMS to be a universal religion, for people everywhere, for all races and classes, with no barriers. Even though there are many different groups within Islam, there is still a noticeable uniformity and unity about their core beliefs and practices. They believe that their religion is very simple, unlike Christianity, which is considered to be intricate. They all practise the same rituals at the same time all over the world. Their religious acts seem to be identical at every point of the compass. Though there are some differences in practice and behaviour, there is a unifying common denominator: one God, Allah, and Muhammad as his Messenger. They pray in the same way, read and recite from the same book (the Qur'an) and even use the same opening passage at every prayer. In prayer, they face the same direction towards the *Ka'aba* (the sacred shrine) in Mecca; they eat the same food (*Halal*, meaning lawful); and they dress and behave in almost the same way. (In Western societies, however, modern, fashionable clothing is often worn.)

Islam comprises both a body of beliefs and a set of religious practices, that is *Iman* (the faith) and *Din* (the religious practices derived from the faith). In order to become a believer *(mumin),* a Muslim has to believe in six articles, five of which are stated in *Surah 4.136:* 'Any who denieth Allah, his angels, his Books, his Messengers, and the Day of Judgment, hath gone far, far astray.' A Muslim must make a public confession of faith with the tongue and believe with the heart (just as Christians are required to do in *Romans 10.9-10).* Even though Muslims are diverse, these fundamentals unite them and are compulsory to all.

Here are the six fundamental and essential articles of belief *(Iman mufassal)* regarded as non-negotiable by Muslims:

I. Allah (God)

Muslims completely and totally believe in the existence of one God, and his name is *Allah.* Like the Bible, the Qur'an does not argue about this or try to prove it. The doctrine of the Trinity, however, is vehemently denied and rejected. Atheism is unknown among Muslims and considered to be a great sin. It is taken for granted that everyone believes in God. Anyone who claims that there is no God is a fool. The Bible teaches the same when the Psalmist says, 'The fool hath said in his heart, There is no God' *(Psalm 14.1; 53.1).*

Their belief in God covers four aspects:

a) The Islamic creed

'There is no God [deity] but Allah, and Muhammad is his Messenger' *(La ilaha ill' Allah Wa Muhammadun rasul Allah).* Every Muslim must believe and confess this simple but absolutely essential creed. It is inculcated from childhood. Muslims will try to persuade a Christian or a Westerner to recite it. It is considered a notable victory when a Westerner is converted to Islam. This confession is said to be *heavier* than the 'seven Heavens and the seven Earths' with all their inhabitants. (Muslims believe that there are seven Heavens and seven layers to earth – *Surah 67.3-5.*) They are absolute monotheists, believing that Allah is a unitary being dwelling alone as 'the One'. The Triune God of the Bible is an anathema to them. The creed is also called *Tawheed* (the oneness of God). Although this expression is not found in the Qur'an, it is central to Islam. Allah has no equal, no partner and, most definitely, no son, so for Muslims to believe in the Christian Trinity is the most terrible of sins. It is a blasphemy, as they insist on thinking it refers to three gods, whatever we may say to the contrary *(Surah 4.171; 5.72).*

One of the shortest chapters and the most recited of all in the Qur'an reads: 'Say: He Allah is one, Allah, the Eternal, Absolute; he begets not, nor is he begotten; and there is none like unto him' *(Surah 112.1-4; Surah 19.88-89).* To associate partners (or a created being) with Allah is the greatest and the only unforgivable sin, called *shirk*; and it carries the death penalty. The killing of a blasphemer is a law of *Jihad* (Holy War) and earns the perpetrator merit with Allah. If one dies as a *mushrik* (one who associates a created being with God) or as a *kafirun* (an unbeliever or infidel), no one in the world, not even Muhammad himself, can intercede with Allah for him. So this means that calling on Muslims to believe in the Lord Jesus is like asking them to commit the unforgivable sin. And for a Muslim 'who changed his religion, kill him', Muhammad said *(Al-Bukhari 84.57).*[6] That is why evangelism and proselytism is prohibited in most Muslim countries. Clearly the fear of committing such a sin and losing all on earth and in the hereafter constitutes the most formidable barrier to conversion which can be imagined. Surely this should draw out our Christian compassion to pray for them and to enlighten their understanding. It is as if Islam has been designed to oppose and deny Christianity in all essential points.

---

6   Imam Al-Bukhari (ninth century): his prolific collection of Hadith is considered by the majority of Muslims worldwide to be one of the most authentic and most reliable.

b) Allah's excellent names

(Surah 7.179; 59.22-24)

The name of *Allah* dominates the Qur'an, and also the life, speech and actions of all Muslims. *Allahu Akbar* means 'Allah is great', *In sha'Allah* means 'If Allah wills', and *Allahu-alam* means 'Only Allah knows'. These are very common expressions for Muslims.

The Qur'an contains the *Asma alhusna,* or the 'Ninety-nine most beautiful names of Allah' (most Muslim boys are named after these). These are the names by which one must approach Allah. A common practice is to recite them with the help of a rosary or prayer beads. It is believed theoretically that whoever does so will definitely enter Heaven. Tradition says there is an exalted 'hundredth name' that only the camels know, which explains their proud look and the fact that Arab Muslims like to own camels. Any person pronouncing this *unknown* name will have all his desires granted. Many things Muslims do and believe, such as this, are not actually in the Qur'an but in the Hadith. However, the truth is that in practice the Qur'an and the Hadith are inseparable – one interprets the other.

For Christians, the great missing divine attribute in the Muslim understanding is the glorious fact that 'God is love', found in the Bible (eg: *John 3.16; 1 John 4.8, 16*). In the Qur'an, Allah is the 'loving one', and the 'beloved one', but love is not ascribed to him as actually inherent in his nature. Similarly, Allah is never called 'Father' in the Qur'an, because he has only slaves not sons, merely chattels not children. A Christian can relate intimately to the Godhead: Father, Son and Holy Spirit; but a Muslim cannot, though Allah is called the 'Merciful One' and the 'Compassionate'.

---

c) Allah's seven attributes

Muslims assign seven great and primary attributes to Allah: *life* (he has no beginning and no end); *knowledge* (he is omniscient – nothing is secret to him); *power* (if he wills, he can make stones and trees to walk); *will* (he permits good and evil to exist by his will);

hearing (he hears without ears); *seeing* (he can see even a black ant on a black stone on a dark night); and *speech* (he speaks without a tongue).

d) Allah's transcendence

Allah holds himself distant from man. He dispenses mercy or punishment at whim. He is unknowable, inaccessible, and beyond any description. Being unitary rather than triune in nature, he cannot be a relational God, as in Christianity. Therefore you can know Allah's law and will, but never his person or his character or his heart. He is a ruler not a friend. He is certainly not a father, for sixteen times the Qur'an says that Allah is not a father and has no son.

2. The Angels (malaikatuhu)

Muslims believe in the existence of angels and of spirits or *Jinns* (demons), who are qualified to be Allah's messengers, with various ranks. They believe that angels are sinless, and that they will die and be raised at the Last Day. They also believe that the angel Gabriel, the illustrious messenger endued with power, transmitted the entire content of the Qur'an through dictation in Arabic to Muhammad in stages over a period of twenty-three years (AD 610-632). It was also Gabriel, as in the Bible, who appeared to Mary (the mother of Jesus Christ, and the only woman mentioned by name in the Qur'an) to announce that she would miraculously give birth to a son *(Surah 19.17)*.

Muslims believe that angels were created from light (whereas the devil was created from fire, and man was created from clay). Their purpose is to obey and carry out Allah's will. It is stated in the Qur'an that when Allah created Adam he commanded the angels to worship him. All of them did so, except *Iblis* (the devil, *Surah 2.34*). His excuse was, 'He [Adam] was made of clay, but I was made of fire. I am better than he, so why should I worship him?' Allah cursed

Iblis (also called *Ash-Shaytan* or Satan) for his disobedience and cast him out of Paradise. He became man's chief enemy, and the head of the demons and evil spirits *(Jinns)*. Adam 'fell' too, through the temptation of Satan; but Adam's fall was quite literal – he fell down from Heaven to earth *(Surah 2.36)*. Because of his disobedience in eating the 'fruit' (a tradition says it was wheat) he was expelled from Heaven. It is taught that Adam was later forgiven and restored as a prophet.

Eight angels are known by name: *Gabriel* (the angel responsible for the transmission of the Qur'an); *Michael* (the patron of the Jews) who brings Allah's prosperity and blessings to man; *Israfil,* responsible for blowing the last trumpet at the Last Day (resurrection and judgement); *Azra'il* (the angel of death); *Malik* (chief angel supervising hell); *Radwan* (responsible for supervising Heaven); *Munkar* and *Nakir* (the examining angels). Eight other angels hold the throne of God, but nineteen guard the gates of hell *(Surah 74.28-30)*; each point of the compass also has guardian angels.

Every person has an angel and a demon appointed over him. They are nearer to him than his 'life vein'. Some believe that men are protected by ten angels day and night. One of the missions of the angels, the Qur'an teaches, is to pray for forgiveness for all on earth *(Surah 42.5)*. *Munkar* and *Nakir* are the two angels that Muslims will encounter soon after death. They record a man's sins and good works on his shoulder-blades. They also question the newly-deceased (regarding their lives and beliefs) as soon as the burial takes place and the mourners have left the graveyard. They will ask four questions of the deceased: Who is your God? Who is your prophet? What is your religion? What is your *Qibla* (direction of Mecca)?

When concluding their prayers, Muslims always turn to the right and to the left to greet these two angels. Muslims always greet each other in the plural – *Assalaam-alaykum*: 'Peace be upon you and the angels beside you.' This also serves as a test to know if a person is a Muslim or not. The word *salaam* means 'peace', but in their understanding real peace can exist only where the Islamic *Sharia* law rules and controls all matters of state and religion.

As well as angels, Allah uses evil spirits or *Jinns* (created from fire free of smoke – *Surah 55.15*). It is believed that these evil spirits dwell in graveyards, empty houses, and by water, blood and ashes. Their possible presence and harmfulness is taken very seriously (especially in folk Islam).

3. The Books (kutubuhu)

(Surah 2.136; 4.136, 163; 32.23; cf. 2.53, 87; 5.46, 48; 11.110; 45.16)

In the Qur'an there are references to the *Torah* (of Moses), the *Suhuf* (books of the Old Testament prophets), the *Zabur* (Psalms of David) and the *Injil* (the New Testament – not just the Gospels). Muslims believe that Allah gave 104 sacred books to mankind. Of these 104, 100 were shared out between Adam (10), Seth (50), Enoch or Idriss (30), and Abraham (10), but they have been lost. The four remaining are the Books of Moses, the Psalms of David, the Gospel of Jesus Christ, and the Qur'an.

The Qur'an is also called in Arabic: *Al-Kitab* (the Book), *Al-Furqan* (the Distinction), *Al-Dikhr* (the Warning), *Al-Mushaf* (the Collection). It is called the blessed, the luminous, and the honourable Book *(Surah 3.184; 6.155; 38.29)*. The Qur'an was sent down from Heaven where it existed from the beginning of time. It is regarded as divine because the prophet Muhammad, who was considered to be illiterate and uneducated, was miraculously able to read it and pass it on *(Surah 43.4; 96.1-5)*.

Muslims claim that Allah has given them a 'two-edged sword' for the cause of Islam in our day – the Qur'an and oil (money). The Qur'an supersedes the Bible. It is the 'wonder of wonders' revealed to Muhammad in a succession of direct revelations, and its wording is letter for letter fixed by Allah, without Muhammad rephrasing any part of it with his own words. When he was asked to do a miracle as proof of his prophethood, he said he had no such power, but instead pointed them to the Qur'an as the matchless miracle of all – even though the Qur'an was not yet put together at that time *(Surah 2.23; 10.37-38; 13.31; 17.88)*. Muslims believe that the Qur'an is a sign or a miracle from Allah, because it was unaltered by man, free from any human input, free from any textual corruption, full of literary beauty, and seen as an unequalled work of literature.

Muslims are taught that the Qur'an has been divinely protected against falsification, whereas the Scriptures written before Muhammad have been changed or corrupted by Christians and Jews (although there is no textual evidence of this). At the same time, and rather strangely, Muslims are told that if they are in doubt about what they have read in the Qur'an, they are to ask the 'People of the Book': Christians and Jews *(Surah 5.68)*.

The Qur'an is shorter than the New Testament. It consists of 114 chapters or *Surahs* (86 of which were revealed to Muhammad while in Mecca and 28 in Medina), and 6,239 (or by another estimate 6,616) verses in total. It is divided into thirty sections, making it easier to memorise and recite during the thirty days of fasting in the sacred month of Ramadan. Each Surah has a name, such as 'The Opening', 'The Cow', 'The House of Imran', and 'Women'. Every chapter of the Qur'an, except *Surah 9*, starts with the phrase, 'In the name of Allah the Merciful, the Compassionate'. Competitions are organised and a financial reward is given to the best memoriser. The prophet encouraged his followers to make their voices sound more beautiful when they read it out loud. When sung, the Qur'an excites their hearts. It is not important to know the meaning of its words; the important thing is to perform it correctly.

To read it, however, is very difficult. The chapters seem to jump back and forth in subject matter. This is why the Qur'an is not self-explanatory (unlike the Bible where there is a logical and progressive record). You need the explanations of the Hadith or Traditions as a means of interpretation, although some statements can be so direct that they don't need to be interpreted, as in *Surah 9.5* and *29.*[7] Muslims look down on the Bible because of its means of inspiration, having been produced by many men over many centuries, as they were moved by the Holy Spirit Who utilised their styles. The Qur'an, they say, was directly dictated from Heaven, so it must be superior because it is wholly divine. Strictly speaking it cannot be 'translated', unlike the Bible; and many Muslims believe that it is impossible for languages other than Arabic to properly express the meaning of the Qur'an.

A Book to Revere

The Islamic teaching is that the divinely revealed Qur'an was received orally and was not compiled as a single book until after Muhammad's death in AD 632. The Qur'an is called *Umm-al Kitab*, 'the Mother of all Books' *(Surah 3.7; 13.39; 43.3-4)* – perfect, uncreated and eternally existent in the seventh Heaven *(Surah 85.21-22)*, and brought down by the angel Gabriel piece by piece to be revealed to Muhammad. Thus the Qur'an is 'faultless, perfect and free from error' and Muslims are commanded to obey every word in the Qur'an and believe in every teaching given by Muhammad *(Surah 4.80; 59.7)*.

The Qur'an as an actual book is treated as sacred and therefore most highly regarded: kissed, placed against the forehead as an act of respect, never laid on the ground, and never held below the waist. 'Surely it is a bounteous book that is protected, which none touches save the purified ones' *(Surah 56.77-79)*. The Qur'an is touched only

---

7 'And when the sacred months have passed, then kill the polytheists wherever you find them and capture them and besiege them and sit in wait for them at every place of ambush. But if they should repent, establish prayer, and give zakat, let them [go] on their way. Indeed, Allah is Forgiving and Merciful.' 'Fight those who do not believe in Allah or in the Last Day and who do not consider unlawful what Allah and his Messenger have made unlawful and who do not adopt the religion of truth from those who were given the Scripture – [fight] until they give the jizyah [tax] willingly while they are humbled.'

after a ritual washing of hands. It must be printed and published in a 'dignified format' – hardbound with a decorated cover, and printed with 'dignified script'. The script must be set apart by framing with special borders; nothing but the verse numbers can be inside the borders. No comments or illustrations can be inside the borders alongside the text. It must always be put on the highest shelf in the house, and never placed with another book on top of it.

A GREATER AND SUPERIOR BOOK TO REVERE: THE BIBLE

- As Christians, we must always treat our Bibles, our 'living book', in a respectful way. But, of course, we do not worship the paper. However, the Bible we use in our witness to Muslims should not be in poor condition, with underlined notes or highlighted verses. It is the Word of God, and contains the words of life. The Qur'an alludes to the Bible hundreds of times, but it is always better and wiser to draw our learning from the Bible itself and not from a secondary source. The Muslims we approach will observe how we treat God's Word and will be put off by any apparent disrespect of it.

- It is worth noting how different the method of biblical inspiration is compared to that claimed for the Qur'an. In the case of the Bible, God used the instrumentality of godly men over centuries providing a remarkable self-authentication of its inspired nature, seen in the agreement of all its parts and the internal fulfilment of so many of its prophecies. The Qur'an, however, was 'channelled' by a spirit-being purporting to be from God, Muhammad being the only recipient and reporter between God and men. Muslims believe that Muhammad was illiterate, but miraculously, when he was commanded to 'read', he could do so *(Surah 7.157-158; 96.1-5)*. It is not easy to accept that Muhammad could not read and write for he was a merchant employed by a wealthy widow who trusted him because of his knowledge and talents in business.

- If the Qur'an is untranslatable, as it is claimed, and should be expressed only in Arabic, then it surely cannot be a message for the whole world. The idea of a 'sacred language' for a world religion is unreasonable. The Bible, however, is a universal book which can be translated into all languages and is still able to make its readers 'wise unto salvation'.

4. The Prophets (nabihu or rusuluhu)

Muslims generally speak of two classes of prophets: *Nabi* (any prophet inspired by God), and *Rasul* (a messenger or an apostle). Twenty-eight messengers and prophets are mentioned by name in the Qur'an *(Surah 4.163)*, twenty-two of whom also appear in the Bible. According to a tradition, there are 124,000 prophets or messengers, but some groups also believe that there are 144,000 of them, plus 315 other messengers or apostles. No one has ever provided a definitive listing of them all. Each major prophet was sent for a period of time to a specific people. There are six major prophets: Adam (the Chosen); Noah (the Preacher); Abraham (*khalil-Allah* or the Friend of God); Moses (God's Spokesman); Jesus (*Khalimatu Allah* or the Word of Allah); and Muhammad himself, the *Rasul-Allah* (the Messenger of Allah), the last and greatest, the 'seal of the prophets' *(Surah 33.40)*. He was a divinely appointed 'Apostle of God', and is given more than 200 other titles in the Qur'an and Hadith. According to Muslims, Jesus Christ was just a prophet to Israel. Interestingly, Muhammad is the only 'major prophet' mentioned in the Qur'an who is not also mentioned anywhere either in the Old or in the New Testament, although Muslims insist he is the 'Prophet' predicted by Moses and the 'Paraclete' or Comforter promised by the Lord Jesus as we shall explain later *(Deuteronomy 18.15; John 14; 16; Surah 7.157; 61.6)*.

5. The Day of Resurrection and Judgement

(Surah 21.47; 39.68; 52.7-27; 69.13-15; 78.17; 88.8-20)

Muslims believe in Heaven *(Al Jannah)* and hell *(An Nar)*, and in the Day of Judgement. It is the Day of Reckoning *(yum al hisab, yum al-din, yum al qiyama)* or Awakening. It will be the Last Day, the Hour and the Encompassing Day.

The Last Day will be heralded by three trumpet blasts. At a time known only to Allah, the first blast will sound and terrify all creatures in Heaven and earth *(Surah 69.13-35; cf. Surah 21.47; 27.87, 89; 81.1-3, 10-14)*. The mountains shall quake *(Surah 27.90)*, the sun shall be folded up *(Surah 81.1)*, and the moon shall be split *(Surah 54.1)*.

At the second blast, all creatures in Heaven and earth will die. At the last blast (forty years later), all the dead will be raised again for the Judgement. It will be a general resurrection of men, angels, *Jinns* (demons), and even animals.

There is a difference of opinion about the length of this 'Day'. Some say 1,000 years based on *Surah 32.5*, and others 50,000 years based on *Surah 70.4*. After the period of waiting, then comes the Judgement. 'Then those whose balance [of good deeds] is heavy – they will attain salvation: but those, whose balance is light, will be those who have lost their souls; in hell they will abide' *(Surah 23.102-103)*.

Each person will be examined from his own 'book of deeds' (predetermined by Allah) in which all his words and actions are recorded. Allah will weigh all his deeds and words in a weighing balance, one pan being over Paradise and the other over hell *(Surah 21.47)*. For Muslims who have not committed great sins, hell will be cool and pleasant. They believe that Muhammad will plead for them, after Adam, Noah, Abraham, Moses and Jesus Christ all refuse to do so. Those to whom Allah chooses to be merciful, because they have enough merits and good works, will go to eternal Heaven. They will receive their 'book of good works' in the right hand. They will dwell for ever by flowing rivers, reclining on silken couches, praising Allah and enjoying heavenly food and drink in the company of dark-eyed maidens ('seventy-two houris'). In Paradise there are rivers of pure water, milk and honey, and delicious wine *(Surah 37.40-49; 47.15; 55.56, 72; 78.33)*. Heaven for Muslims is an alluring extension of earthly indulgences and whims, particularly attractive to men. It is believed that even the lowliest Muslim will enjoy prolonged pleasure for a thousand years and his enjoyment will increase a hundredfold. One wonders how it is that Allah can forbid something on earth and yet give it in abundance in Heaven, such as rivers of wine.

All this contradicts the words of Christ, Who said that in Heaven there will be no marriage; instead men and women will be like angels *(Matthew 22.30)*. The Islamic Heaven makes Muslims' mouths water (especially those of men) with its desirable and sensual promises.

Those whose scale is light *(Surah 7.8-9)* and those whom Allah rejects will abide in the fires of hell for ever – in eternal perdition, they will drink from a boiling spring and eat bitter thorny plants which neither nourish nor relieve hunger *(Surah 56.42-43; 88.4-7)*. These will receive their 'book of good works' in their left hand. Hell is the destiny of all who do not accept Islam *(Surah 14.34; 18.28; 20.76)*. One does not know until the Day of Judgement whether one is to go to hell or to Paradise. It is commonly believed that Muhammad will intercede for Muslims on that Day.

A WORD ABOUT WOMEN IN ISLAM (SURAH 4.34)

Muhammad's teaching about women reflected many of the ideas of his day. He said that women are a 'field' and a 'plaything' *(Surah 2.223)*. They are, by nature, unclean and only half as intelligent as men (a tradition from the *Hadith 3.826; 2.541*). He believed that women are both more deficient in intelligence and in religion than men, and that the testimony of a woman is equal to only half that of a man, and a woman inherits half of a man's share for men are superior *(Surah 4.11; cf. 2.282)*. They are forbidden to marry a non-Muslim whereas a Muslim man can marry a Christian (with the aim to convert her to Islam). The prophet was asked about hell's inhabitants, and he replied, 'I also saw the hell-fire and I had never seen such a horrible sight. I saw that most of the inhabitants were women' (a Hadith reported by Sahih Al-Bukhari *1.28, 301; 2.161; 7.124*). There is no description of women enjoying Heaven in the Qur'an. He said that women could be beaten (as a last resort) if they did not fully obey their husbands in everything *(Surah 4.34)*. He also said that the day women were in power would be the end of the world.

Muhammad married a minimum of twelve wives, one of whom was only nine years old (according to a Hadith), and took two concubines. In all that he did, he claimed to have received a special revelation from Allah.

It is reported that Aisha, his youngest wife, taunted him in a jealous show-down saying, 'Your God indeed rushes in coming to fulfil your desires.' She also complained once by saying: 'It is not good that you people have made us equal to dogs and donkeys' *(Hadith 1.498)*. His first wife (a wealthy widow named Khadija) is thought to be in Heaven near Mary, the mother of the Lord Jesus, and with Asva, Pharaoh's wife who (according to the Qur'an) saved Moses from the waters. According to a Hadith, Muhammad said, 'Mary is the best woman in the world, and Khadija is the best of this nation.' In fairness, he was faithful to Khadija (her uncle was a nominal Christian) until her death, when he started to take multiple wives. So while his first wife was alive, Muhammad was not a polygamist. Two months after Khadija's death he took Sawda as a wife and betrothed Aisha, six years of age, and married her officially three years later. Islam teaches that a man can have up to four wives at a time, but only as he is able to care for them equally in terms of finances and affection *(Surah 4.3)*. Husbands may divorce their wives at any time for the slightest reason, but women have no legal right to divorce. A husband needs only to say three times, 'I divorce you', and that is it. Nevertheless full divorce takes place after a three-month waiting period to seek reconciliation, or to see if the woman is pregnant with a child he may then claim.

In general, Muslim women are always under the protection of a man – a husband, a father, or another male relative. Their 'honour' is of paramount importance to the good name of the family. Any suggestion of dishonour may lead to an 'honour killing', even in the West. There is some variation in the amount of individual freedom a woman can enjoy, depending on the regional culture.

6. Destiny or fate: Al-Qadar or predestination
(Surah 2.284; 6.39; 14.4; 35.8; 74.31; 76.29-30)

Muslims believe that Allah is the direct author of both good and evil *(Surah 113.1-2)*. Islamic predestination is not at all like biblical predestination. Rather it is a kind of inescapable fatalism, and places the responsibility for all that a man does, whether good or evil, upon Allah entirely. God is in effect the author of evil. 'Allah verily sendeth astray whom he will, and whom he will he guides' *(Surah 35.8)*. 'Your fate is fastened to your neck' *(Surah 17.13)*. 'The future is past,' because all is settled in advance; thus men cannot be held responsible for their actions, and yet illogically there will still be a great day of accountability or judgement. It is believed that after forty days in the womb, an angel writes out your whole life story, through to the day of your death, which is then written on your forehead at birth. He also records if you are going to Heaven or to hell.

It is the devil's touch that makes the child cry out at birth. One must accept one's fate with resignation. Luck, chance, accident, misfortune, failure are all ascribed to the will of Allah. It is *mektub* (written). Every man has his written scroll. A tradition says that Allah wrote the fate of all creation fifty thousand years before he created the Heavens and the earth. So do not be surprised when a Muslim doesn't say, 'Thank you' when he is given something. As long as he says, 'Thank you' to Allah, that is enough. Allah determined or fixed what you gave! As will be explained in a later section, only martyrdom in the cause of Holy War can guarantee Paradise. Yet this is all in Allah's will too, and some say even in the case of martyrdom absolute certainty is not possible, because Allah's will is inscrutable and he may do as he wishes.

WHAT DO MUSLIMS PRACTISE?

MUSLIM PRACTICES (personal and corporate) are regulated down to the smallest detail. There are *Five Pillars* that hold up the 'House of Islam' *(Dar-Al-Islam)* and on which their faith rests. These are five compulsory obligations *(fard)* or practical duties (found in the Qur'an and the Hadith), which every good Muslim must carry out.

1. Confession of faith (The Shahadah or the Kalima)

The first pillar is the reciting frequently of the Muslim creed (the shortest of any religion): *'La ilaha illa Allah, Wa Muhammadun rasul Allah'* ('There is no God [deity] but Allah, and Muhammad is his Messenger'). It has just eight words in the Arabic; though they do not actually appear in the Qur'an in this form. The first part is found several times in the Qur'an, but the second has been added by the Hadith (Traditions). The *Shahadah* means literally, 'to bear witness'. This is the foundation and the profession which unites the Muslim world. It is the cornerstone of the Islamic faith, the simplest and the most repeated creed in the world. Almost everyone has heard of it. The reciting of the confession of faith is the key thing *(Surah 37.35; 47.19; 48.29)*. No one can become a Muslim without it. It is the *easy-believism* formula for a proselyte. To actually become a Muslim it must be said, for the first time, in Arabic (the sacred language) with conviction and before witnesses (ideally in a mosque). This confession appears on the Saudi Arabian flag. It is inscribed in many mosques (including the Dome of the Rock in Jerusalem); on doorposts; used as a battle cry; as a 'motto text' whispered to the new-born baby in the right then the left ear; as a naming formula to welcome the child into the world (the shaving of the head ceremony after seven days) and to be a means of protection; and spoken in the ears of the dying. Many will also chant it and use it simply as a charm, believing it will drive away evil. Alongside various chapters and verses of the Qur'an, it is recited to resolve problems such as fevers and toothache; and reciting the creed and portions of the Qur'an is considered to be a 'good luck' activity and a personal protection.

2. Prayers (Salat)

Memorised and unvarying prayers are recited at fixed times every day. Prayer is more of a ritual than a close fellowship with God. Every gesture in prayer illustrates one's deep submission to the will of Allah. The devout Muslim must pray five times daily facing the *Qibla* or *Ka'aba* (in the direction of Mecca), wherever he happens to be in the world. The prayers must be performed according to a prescribed ritual. A Muslim is very proud of his prayer routine, regarding Christians as virtually prayerless in comparison.

Even though there is not a single verse in the Qur'an where all five prayer times are mentioned together, they are not optional *(Surah 11.114)*. The Muslim is obligated to pray five times a day: at daybreak, then just before noon, in the afternoon, *after* sunset (so it will not seem that he is worshipping the sun), and finally at night-fall. All these prayers must be recited in Arabic.

In Muslim countries and sometimes elsewhere, the call to prayer is sounded by a *muezzin* (prayer-crier) from a tower called a mina-ret, part of the public place of worship – the mosque. The early morning prayer before dawn wakes the worshippers with these words (spoken aloud every single morning): 'God is great! God is great! Confess that there is no God but Allah. Confess that there is no God but Allah. Confess that Muhammad is his prophet. Confess that Muhammad is his prophet. Testify that there is no God but Allah, and that Muhammad is his Messenger. Oh, slaves of Allah give life to prayer, for prayer is better than sleep.'

Muslims (especially men) are required to worship in a mosque each Friday – which earns twenty-five times more merit than a prayer in one's own house or elsewhere. Friday is the Muslims' holy day and most blessed of all days. It is the day on which the sun was created; on which Adam was created; and on which the Last Day will occur. It is not a day of spiritual and physical rest, as with Sunday for Christians; but the peace of the world supposedly hangs on what the *Imam* (cleric) says on a Friday. However, so often for Muslims, emerging from mosques after a vitriolic sermon, Friday is definitely not the most peaceful of days.

Before praying, a Muslim must perform a purification ritual: he must wash his feet, hands and parts of his face *(Surah 2.136-145; 5.6)*, including the nose; it is believed that the devil spends the night inside a person's nose (a well-known Muslim Hadith). Where water is not available, dry ablutions with sand or earth may be substituted. There is no personal prayer, but instead a recitation of set words. Prayer involves standing, bowing, kneeling, prostration (hands and face on the ground) and sitting (seventeen rounds are performed in each prayer and the *Fatihah*, the opening chapter of the Qur'an and the pattern prayer, is repeated thirty-two times in a day). Most

Muslims do not speak Arabic, but need to memorise two or three Surahs for their daily ritual and as a means of protection. Women may also gather at the mosque on Fridays, but they generally pray out of sight of the men. These prayers, we emphasise, are the recitation of prescribed words in Arabic to be memorised, and the non-Arab often does not understand what he is reciting. In fact there are many Arabs who do not understand the Arabic used in the Qur'an, but they take everything they read in it at face value.

Muslims also offer prayers for the dead and ask dead 'saints' to intercede for them. Children (boys and girls) must start to learn to pray at seven years of age, and by the age of ten the children must be forced to pray by means of admonition from parents.

The very manner of prayer (particularly prostration) is intended to show a master-slave relationship, an ongoing and perpetual public and private subjection. Such daily repetition and self-abasement is supposed to make Muslims remember Allah and his greatness. Many Muslims believe that Christians do not pray, or only on Sundays, so we should not feel embarrassed to pray when we are in their company (for example, before meals when we are their guests or they are our guests). We should also remember what the Lord taught about prayer in *Matthew 6.5-13*, about not being like the hypocrites who use many and vain words. There can be no way for a Christian to join Muslims in their prayers, or to attend a mosque if invited. The differences between Christian and Muslim prayers are enormous.

The Muslim needs to be respectfully reminded that we do not perform any ritual or ablutions because it is the heart which needs cleansing, not the body – 'the blood of Jesus Christ his Son cleanseth us from all sin' *(1 John 1.7; cf. Jeremiah 17.9).*

3. Almsgiving or the poor tax (Zakat)

Muslims are required to give 2.5% (one fortieth) of their personal income or wealth to the poor and needy, but only those of the 'House of Islam' *(Surah 64.16; 98.5).* It is a key part of salvation by good works. The believer should expect unfathomable blessings as he pays it *(Surah 2.110, 277).* The *Zakat* is paid once a year out of one's carefully calculated annual, not accumulated, savings. Many consider it just a religious duty and give it without compassion. The purpose is to give relief to the Muslim poor. It is also given to the collectors of *Zakat*, to new converts, to prisoners (for release or ransom), to debtors, to needy travellers and to the *Mujahidin* (those who are serving to spread Islam, or fighting for Allah). The money is also used to build mosques, schools and hospitals, but not for paying the clergy. It is generally not given to non-Muslims. The linking of almsgiving with spiritual reward must surely lead to the giver being motivated by gain in the sight of Allah, not benevolence.

Christian charity is characteristically universal. Christians must support members of their own families and brethren who are in need, but their charity should extend more widely *(Galatians 6.9-10; 1 Timothy 5.8)*. Muslim charity as a communal requirement is certainly not universal, as we see from the difficulties Christians in Muslim countries face in obtaining aid in times of crisis. The motto, 'Love for all, hatred for none' is for the West, and is not a reality in Muslim nations.

4. Fasting (Saum)

'Oh you who believe, fasting is prescribed for those before you, so that you may guard against evil' *(Surah 2.183-185)*.

The famous fasting month of Ramadan is the ninth month of the Islamic calendar. It moves forward some nine to eleven days each year (as the Islamic calendar is lunar rather than solar), and its timing is a frequent cause of dispute between Muslims. There is often a twenty-four hour time difference. The beginning of Ramadan commemorates the day when Muhammad received his first revelation from the angel Gabriel, when he then fasted; so in honour to him, Muslims do so also. During Ramadan, the gates of Heaven are open and prayers are carried straight to the throne of God. It is a month in which particularly great veneration is due to Muhammad.

Fasting is compulsory from sunrise to sunset, sunrise being the time when it becomes possible to distinguish between a white and a black thread *(Surah 2.187)*. The fast lasts twenty-nine to thirty days, and is defined as total abstinence from food, drink, tobacco, perfumes, and conjugal relations during daylight hours. It is obligatory for all from the age of about ten years *(Surah 2.183-187)*. The sick, the disabled, travellers, *jihadists* (those involved in Holy War), pregnant women and nursing mothers, are all usually exempt, but must catch up or 'pay back' by fasting later on in the year. The elderly are also exempt, but must offer a sacrifice: a meal a day to be paid to charity in kind or cash. During this period even one's own saliva should not be swallowed, a challenge to even the most zealous. After sunset and before dawn, a Muslim can eat and drink as much as he likes.

It is an arduous month for many, but not for the rich who can stay in their homes and sleep through the day. It is a month of great religiosity but also of much quarrelling because of frayed tempers. In many countries, especially if it coincides with the heat of summer, the pace of life has to slow down. It is the month most Muslims end up spending the most money and gaining the most weight, because after sunset fasting is typically replaced by over-indulgence. There is more food sold (and more feasting) during Ramadan than during any other month of the year. Yet in some Muslim nations restaurants will be closed, for it is against the law to eat or drink in public during the fast. This month-long fast is seen as one of the vital good works that can gain admission to Paradise.

The subject of fasting is a good bridge in talking with Muslims *(Isaiah 58; Mark 7.15-23)*, but it is best not to be too 'challenging' during these days, as some may become very 'religious', zealous, and disinclined to hear.

5. Pilgrimage (Hajj) to Mecca
(Surah 2.189, 196-198; 22.27-30)

Hajj means to 'make one's way' towards Mecca or Allah. It can also mean 'foreigner' (alien to the holy city – Mecca). Each Muslim (male or female) is expected to make a seven-day pilgrimage to Mecca (Muhammad's place of birth) at least once in their lifetime *(Surah 22.27-30; 3.97)* if it is physically and financially possible. 'And proclaim to men the pilgrimage: they will come to thee on foot and on every lean camel, coming from every remote path' *(Surah 22.27)*. The sight of *Hajj* is truly an extraordinary one, especially to Western eyes, and fills a Muslim's heart with unparalleled joy and religious fervour. It is one of the greatest religious spectacles on earth. The pilgrimage must be made in the twelfth month of the Muslim calendar (seventy days after Ramadan). The pilgrim is expected to make a seven-fold circumambulation (walk around) of the *Ka'aba* (meaning 'Cube'). The *Ka'aba* is the most sacred shrine of Islam, and is believed to have been built first by Adam, then rebuilt by Abraham while on a visit to his son Ishmael. There is no historical evidence to support this tradition. The Bible record does not place Abraham anywhere near Arabia.

The pilgrim is then to kiss the black stone lodged in its wall, reputedly given to Abraham by the angel Gabriel, and to have fallen down from Heaven. At one of its corners ('the Yemenite corner'), seventy angels are believed to say 'Amen' to the prayers of the pilgrims.

Before going home, the Muslim visits the tomb of Muhammad at Medina. After all this, he is known and respected as *El-Hajj* or *Hajji*, one who has been on *Hajj*, and can return home as pure from sin as the day he was born (as tradition has it). Women are allowed to make the pilgrimage only if they are accompanied by their husband, or by another male adult family member as protector. This is thought to be a good deed on the part of the man and will be rewarded on the Day of Judgement. Muslims are not prohibited from making a pilgrimage at other times of the year too, which is called *Umrah*.

6. The Holy War or Jihad

Many Muslims would add a sixth pillar, considered to be the most notorious practice: the Holy War, the obligation upon every Muslim (especially the young men) to fight against infidels *(Surah 9.5)*. Today the term *Jihad* strikes dread into Westerners. The prophet of Islam ordered that they should make war on men till they said, 'There is no God but Allah.'

Muhammad was once asked: 'What is the best deed?' He replied: 'To believe in Allah and his prophet.' The questioner then asked: 'What is the next [in goodness]?' He replied: 'To participate in Jihad [religious fighting] in Allah's cause' (a tradition narrated by *Abu Huraira 1.25*). 'Jihad will go on until the Day of Judgement' *(Abu Dawood, 15.2484)*.

The Holy War is inscribed on the very heart of Islam and was instrumental in its spectacular early success. For some it is a call to arms only to *defend* Islam. For others, increasingly today, it is a *literal* command to conquer the non-Muslim nations and establish a Muslim state across the whole world, whatever the cost in blood and misery. Soon after Muhammad's death, Abu Bakr led Muslim armies to conquer the Arabian Peninsula, North Africa, Spain, India, and Asia.

The Muslim community around the world is called *Dar-Al-Islam* (House of Islam) and the rest of the world is named *Dar-Al-Harb* (House of the Sword, ie: war). Islam speaks thus about two houses: 'If you are not in the House of Peace *(Dar-Assalam)*, then you are in the House of War,' which is the state of all non-Muslims. Everyone must be brought into the House of Islam for peace to prevail in the world. Unlike Christianity, Islam was born from and spread by the sword, whilst the Lord Jesus commanded His disciples to put away their swords.

Islam sees itself most definitely as the religion *par excellence* of peace and goodwill, resorting to warfare and armed struggle only when the religion itself is under threat *(Surah 2.190-193)*. Since the 1970s this peace and goodwill ideal has been made to seem very hollow by the rise of aggressive Islamic fundamentalism and the advent of the suicide bomber.

The Holy War has two meanings in Islam. One is to strive spiritually, or to struggle for personal holiness by fighting sin; the other is to literally fight for the cause of Islam. There are more than a hundred verses in the Qur'an commanding Muslims to spread Islam with the sword, ie: by subjugation of others, and to impose by force the Islamic faith and rule *(sharia)* on the world. Historically, it was conversion to Islam or death. Confusingly, on the other hand, the Qur'an clearly states: 'Let there be no compulsion in religion' *(Surah 2.256; 4.82)*, cancelled out by 'Kill those who join other gods' *(Surah 9.5)*. The purpose of Jihad is to advance Islam in the world. Engaging in Jihad gives automatic entrance to Paradise at death, especially if there is martyrdom.

A Muslim suicide bomber kills himself to kill others, whilst a Christian is ready to give his life to bring others to the Lord to be saved. Far more Muslims than non-Muslims have been victims of Muslim fundamentalists. Bombing is almost a weekly occurrence in Afghanistan and Pakistan. Jihad brings fear and destabilises whole nations.

Making peace is only considered in Qur'anic terms. For the fundamentalist, the Qur'an does not need to be 'interpreted'; it means what it says and there is no need to soften it. The line between radical and tolerant Islam can easily become blurred. Muslims keep a low profile in the West because as the saying has it: 'If you cannot chop off the hand of your enemy, then kiss it.' But the idea of a peaceful or 'moderate' Muslim is nowhere in the Qur'an. A Muslim peacemaker has no part in Heaven *(Surah 4.95; 5.33)*. Authentic Islam is militant. There is no mercy on those who convert from Islam to Christianity; they must be killed: 'Seize them and kill them wherever you find them' *(Surah 4.89, 91)*. So Muslims are only following what their prophet did. Muhammad urged the use of the sword on his behalf and for the sake of Allah, and he expressly commanded Jihad against his and Allah's enemies: especially Christians and Jews, the so-called 'People of the Book' in the Qur'an *(Surah 2.136, 285; 3.113-115;*

4.74, 136, 163; 5.46; 8.65; 61.4), although punishment varies between Muslim nations in practice.

Muslims often speak about the medieval Christian Crusades in the Holy Land as if all Christians are guilty of violence. To hear them, you would think these events happened only yesterday. There is not a single verse in the Bible to justify what the Crusaders did, for the Bible gives no warrant to spread the faith by violence. The Lord Jesus Christ never asked to be defended with weapons or armies, quite the contrary; whereas with the Qur'an, Jihadists are doing what their holy book explicitly tells them to do. It is a command for them to be engaged in the Holy War, which is not the case for Christians. Muslims are commanded to impose the faith, to fight, and to kill the enemies of Islam, while the Christian faith uses only peaceful and pacific means. We are to preach the Gospel by persuading men and women, but never by imposition or inquisition.

Threats of violence are used by Muslims to intimidate so-called 'infidels'. When Muhammad started preaching about Islam in Mecca he was conciliatory and appeasing to Christians. He told them: 'We believe in what has been sent down to us and sent down to you, our God is the same as your God' *(Surah 29.46)*. However, in Medina, after gaining strength and when the Christians refused to follow Allah, Muhammad was told: 'Fight those who believe not in God nor the last day...Nor acknowledge the religion of truth [Islam], [even if they are] of the people of the Book, until they pay Jizya [tribute tax] with willing submission, and feel themselves subdued' *(Surah 9.29)*. Jihad is the ultimate and most chilling expression of Islam's central doctrine of total surrender.

It is reported that on his deathbed Muhammad requested that his followers ensure that not a single Jew or Christian remained in the Arabian Peninsula, as the birthplace of Islam must be inhabited by Muslims only *(Hadith Al-Bukhari 5.716)*. To this day you will not find a church or a synagogue in Saudi Arabia, the great guardian of Mecca and Medina.

In summary, earning merit with Allah lies at the heart of Islam. The glorious biblical doctrine of grace has no place in Islam. Favour with Allah is all by works. When engaging with Muslims it is vital to remember that it is incredibly hard for them to abandon the security of a lifetime's laboriously acquired merit in order to put their trust in the Saviour.

PART 2

WHAT MUSLIMS BELIEVE ABOUT THE CHRISTIAN FAITH

THERE ARE MANY details in the Qur'an concerning biblical characters which are inaccurate, and there are many passages that flatly contradict the Bible and its message. It is not our purpose to expose all such errors, but it may be helpful to mention a few.

- Abraham offered Ishmael, rather than Isaac, in order to justify Muhammad's prophethood as his coming descendant. This is more than just a mere historical error or a twist of the facts. It is an 'axe laid at the root of the tree' of biblical doctrine and redemption history *(Genesis 22)*. Muhammad insisted that Allah revealed to him that it was Ishmael, not Isaac, who was used to test Abraham's faith *(Surah 37.100-106)*.

- Noah's wife perished with one of her sons during the Flood *(Surah 11.42-43; cf. Genesis 7.13; 1 Peter 3.20)*.

- Haman, the Amalekite, the great enemy of the Jews in the book of *Esther (3.1)*, is portrayed in the Qur'an as Pharaoh's minister *(Surah 8.38)*, even though the events of *Esther* occurred under the Persian Empire in the fifth century BC when Egypt's power had long since declined. (The Pharaoh of the Exodus lived over 900 years before Esther.)

- It was Pharaoh's wife, not his daughter, who adopted Moses *(Surah 28.8-9; cf. Exodus 2.5)*.
- Solomon spoke to birds and could understand the speech of ants *(Surah 27.15-20)*.
- King Saul is confused with Gideon who had 300 warriors *(Surah 2.249; cf. Judges 7.1-7)*.
- According to the Qur'an, Mary gave birth to the Lord Jesus under a palm tree *(Surah 19.23; cf. Luke 2.1-14)*.
- The Qur'an claims that all Christ's disciples were Muslims! *(Surah 5.111)*.
- In the Qur'an, Zechariah, the father of John the Baptist, was dumb for three nights only; but in the Bible he was dumb until the child was born, which was the entire period of Elisabeth's pregnancy *(Surah 3.38-41; 19.16-34; cf. Luke 1.20, 57-64)*.

Many of the errors concerning the Bible and Christianity in the Qur'an are based on erroneous teachings promulgated by heretical Christians with whom Muhammad came into contact in his business travels. This is the tragic result of the true Gospel not being preached and people not being presented with the true faith, making them vulnerable to all sorts of lies and misrepresentations of the truth.

This does not mean we should belittle Muslims. Rather, we should endeavour in every possible way to win them by communicating to them the Good News of the coming of God's Son, the Lord Jesus, to earth. Our weapons are not carnal but spiritual, by the enabling power of the Holy Spirit *(2 Corinthians 10.4-5; cf. Ephesians 6.11-18)*. It may be that Muslims are hard to reach, but it is equally true that many churches have just ignored them. The following chapters present some arguments (there is nothing new under the sun) that Muslims use against Christianity, along with a Christian response.

1. Salvation – What Muslims Think

THE BIBLE exposes our helplessness to save ourselves, as in *Isaiah 64.6* – 'But we are all as an unclean thing, and all our righteousnesses are as filthy rags; and we all do fade as a leaf; and our iniquities, like the wind, have taken us away.' But then it gloriously reveals a free and undeserved salvation through the substitutionary death of the Lord Jesus Christ on the cross of Calvary. God is the Giver *(John 3.16; Ephesians 2.8-10)*.

Muhammad, on the other hand, had no certainty of salvation – 'By Allah, though I am the apostle of Allah, yet I do not know what Allah will do to me' *(Surah 46.9; Hadith 5.58, 266)*.

Islam leaves the world unsaved. No Muslim can ever be sure of his salvation, not even Muhammad: 'nor do I know what will be done with me or with you [my followers]…' *(Surah 46.9; cf. 32.17-18)*. His followers are left hopeless, completely uncertain about their fate until the Day of Judgement. Salvation is summed up in one expression: *Insha'Allah*, 'If Allah wills' *(Surah 18.23-24)*. Allah has not committed himself to anyone. Unlike the God of the Bible, Allah is not a covenant-keeping God, that is, a God Who makes and keeps relational promises, but is a being of arbitrary and total power, whose inscrutable will cannot be known or predicted. There is no personal conversion in Islam. Everyone is trying his best, and must strive alone.

Muslims do not believe that Adam was the 'federal head' or representative of all mankind in his Fall. Adam just made a mistake, for he had forgotten God's command not to eat of the tree. He erred, but then repented, and then all was well. Man is born good, but weak. He is not sinful by nature, only 'sick'. His state is the same both before and after the Fall. He is not inwardly corrupt and does not have a fallen nature. It follows that there is no such thing as original sin in Islam. Man's present state of separation from God is due to God's transcendence, not man's moral fall or depravity. Man's basic problem is ignorance, not sin. Sin for Islam is just a mistake, a slip because God created man weak *(Surah 4.28)*.

How different the Muslim view is from what we read in the Bible about our sinful corruption. 'From the sole of the foot even unto the head there is no soundness in it; but wounds, and bruises, and putrifying sores: they have not been closed, neither bound up, neither mollified with ointment' *(Isaiah 1.6)*. This sorry picture is amplified by the apostle Paul in *Romans 3.10-23*. The Bible clearly says that all men and women are born lost and guilty, and remain so the rest of their lives unless they turn to the Lord Jesus Christ, and find salvation in His precious blood, shed on the cross of Calvary *(John 3.18; 20.30-31; Acts 4.12)*.

In the Bible the plan of salvation is logical and understandable with the help of the Holy Spirit. But the idea of salvation by grace is foreign to Islam, for Islam has no Gospel, no Good News, and no record or account of a redemptive work of God to save men and women. Since Allah is aloof and detached from the human race, there is neither salvation nor assurance of salvation. There is no concept of redemption or substitution to be found in the Qur'an. Such terms are foreign to the Qur'an. Islam denies that there can be any ransom for sinners *(Surah 2.45; 4.157)*. 'No bearer of burdens can bear the burden of another' *(Surah 39.7)*. There is no atonement or reconciliation of the sinner to God by means of the sacrifice of Jesus Christ, or any other sacrifice *(Surah 22.36-37)*. It is supposed that no believer *(mumin)*, who has made a confession of faith, can be lost forever, but such a belief is based on pious tradition and is nowhere found in the Qur'an. On the contrary, the whole tendency of the Qur'an is to suggest how uncertain the position of a believer is before a deity whose leading characteristics are power and inscrutable will.

Salvation in Islam is by good works outweighing evil deeds *(Surah 2.23; 19.96)*. It is all about trying, rather than about faith alone and grace. Heaven must be gained by keeping rules and regulations. There is no way to know except through Jihad, martyrdom, or dying while going or coming back from the *Hajj*. However, the Bible teaches that it is impossible to earn entry into Heaven by good works *(Galatians 2.16; Ephesians 2.8-10)* or by martyrdom *(1 Corinthians 13.3)*. God does not merely require the individual 'to be good' in order to be saved, He requires him to be absolutely and totally perfect. But, of course, no one is capable of perfection *(Romans 3.10-23)*. It is a great but all too common mistake to think that one can compensate for sins by doing good works. God is holy and therefore sin must be paid for. We need the justifying grace of God, as displayed in the atoning sacrifice of Christ. The only way is to come to Him by repenting of sin and seeking forgiveness by His grace. Without this, the doors of Heaven will be shut forever. Heaven is too pure and precious to be 'bought' by anything we might offer or do.

Speaking with Muslims about redemption and forgiveness of sin through the sacrifice of Christ requires forethought and prayer. Even the most faithful Muslims do not know where they will spend eternity (except such as martyrs. Interestingly, Muhammad did not die as a martyr, meaning he is not yet saved, but lives only in an intermediate state.)

What an assurance for Christians that we can know where we will be after death! 'We know' is the unparalleled Christian statement of faith *(1 John 2.3)*. Christ's work on the cross of Calvary made Heaven certain. For Christians, salvation is *obtaining*, rather than *attaining*. It is *receiving*, rather than *achieving*. It is *trusting*, rather than *trying*, because salvation has already been achieved for us, and is completely finished *(John 19.30)*.

- Point out to Muslims that the problem facing man is the problem of his heart: 'The heart is deceitful above all things, and desperately wicked' *(Jeremiah 17.9)*. All that Muslims do and the way they behave is an instinctive spiritual cry for the forgiveness of their sins, but tragically they are knocking at the wrong door. Indeed they are burdened and heavy laden by sin, zealous to earn Heaven and avoid hell. We need to keep on speaking to them about sin and how Christ came in great compassion to seek and save that which was lost *(Luke 19.10)*. Cornelius was perhaps similar to a 'good' Muslim. He had sincere religious beliefs and practices, but he was missing something essential and Someone special, the Lord Jesus Christ. Peter had to visit his home and explain Christ's offer of salvation to him *(Acts 10)*.

- When we tell Muslims about Heaven, they are likely to ask: Can one know for sure? There are so many verses in the Bible that speak about the reality of a believer in Christ entering Heaven *(Luke 10.20; Philippians 4.3)*. We can give the example of the repentant thief crucified alongside Christ. The Lord Jesus said to him: 'Verily I say unto thee, To day shalt thou be with me in paradise' *(Luke 23.43)*. C. H. Spurgeon once said, in his inimitable way: 'If we do not get to Heaven before we die, we will never get there.' Christ Himself said: 'I am the way, the truth, and the life' *(John 14.6)*. Paul wrote that there is 'one mediator between

God and men, the man Christ Jesus' *(1 Timothy 2.5; cf. Hebrews 7.24-25)*.

- Be careful to clearly explain that our certainty of salvation by grace is not a licence to sin. Muslims think that if a person knew that he had a place in Heaven, he would live as he liked. However, in the Bible grace leads to holiness – we actually *want* to be holy *(Romans 6.1ff; Hebrews 12.14; James 2.20-26)*. We strive to overcome sin. We cannot be indifferent to it. We live according to what we believe. There is a link between what we believe and our behaviour. When there is consistency between our talk and our walk, others, including Muslims, notice it.

- Explain that God is not a distant God. We can seek and find Him *(Matthew 6.33; 7.7-11)*. God spiritually reveals Himself to those who seek Him with all their heart. There are no rituals or ceremonies required to approach Him. We are able to come before the throne of grace because Christ's sacrifice has met all the requirements of God's righteousness. God can be known through His Son *(Matthew 11.25-30)*. The Bible describes God as 'our Father' – a term with which we are all familiar – but God's love is far greater than an earthly father's. True worship is about what goes on inside the heart and the mind. It is not about what we eat or drink, but about what comes out from the mouth *(Matthew 15.11; Mark 7.20-23)*.

- Show that salvation is much more than saying: 'I believe in God', or, 'There is only one God', for the devil also knows these things and trembles *(James 2.19)*. Sincere belief does not make something true; a person can be sincere and yet be terribly wrong.

2. The Trinity – the Muslim Dilemma

CHRISTIANS BELIEVE IN one God who is Triune (three-in-oneness); Muslims are unitarians – Allah is a solitary, unitary being, absolutely One and nothing else. The Bible teaches that while God is One, He exists in three distinct co-equal Persons – Father, Son and Holy Spirit. While the word 'Trinity' is a theological term and not itself in the Bible, the reality of it is clearly taught. It is a humbling and overwhelming fact to know that the Creator God has revealed Himself to our humankind. This is how God has chosen to reveal Himself to us in His Word and we accept this revelation by faith. The devout Muslim says, 'How can He be Three in One and One in Three? Allah will not forgive the Trinitarians' *(Surah 4.48; 28.62-64)*.

The concept of the Trinity is certainly difficult to fully understand – which only tends to confirm that it was not an idea concocted by man. The Islamic distortion of the Trinity is: 'God (the Father), Mary (His consort) and Jesus (the Son)' *(Surah 5.73-75, 116-117)*.

In the Qur'an, the Lord Jesus was asked by Allah if He ever said that He is the Son of God, which He 'denied' *(Surah 5.72-73, 116; 6.101; cf. Surah 4.156-158, 171)*. It is sadly true that there were so-called 'Christians' in Muhammad's time who worshipped Mary (as many still do), but no such concept of the Trinity is to be found anywhere in the Bible, and was never held by any biblical Christians at any time, then or now.

Why such a misunderstanding? Before Muhammad claimed to be a prophet, he travelled extensively with his uncle as a trader. In those travels he encountered heretical Christian sects (the Nestorians, the Monophysites, etc) scattered throughout the Arabian Peninsula. He saw many idols, shrines, crosses, crucifixes, and the Holy Spirit represented as a dove, along with various other 'Christian' symbols. One thing he certainly noticed among the idols was a venerated woman holding a baby, which may have led him to think that the Trinity was an idolatrous 'polytheistic' deity, namely God (the Father), Mary (the Mother) and Jesus (the Son).

Ordinary Muslims have often thought that Christians worship three gods. Unfortunately, although Muslim scholars understand the orthodox Christian belief about the Trinity, they allow this popular misconception to flourish amongst the Muslim masses. It must be noted also that the Qur'an never uses the word 'Trinity', but says, 'Say not three.' So Islam has reacted against wrong, idolatrous beliefs and practices, not against the *biblical* and orthodox view of the Trinity, of which Muhammad seems to have been unaware.

Surah 112 is just four verses (recited every day by at least a billion Muslims), but is particularly notable on account of the Trinity, as it is at great pains to emphasise the absolute *unity* of God (Allah), and that he cannot possibly 'beget' (meaning he cannot have a son).

We must consistently disown these distortions of the true Trinitarian doctrine, explaining that the title 'Son of God' refers to a spiritual 'sonship', not a physical or biological one. No true Christian has or would ever hold to such an idea. No Christian believes that

God fathered a son through a woman called Mary, reducing God to our human level! God from all eternity existed in three Persons – Father, Son, and Holy Spirit – the same in substance, or in essence, and equal in power, glory, and eternal existence. As the hymnwriter puts it:

> *Almighty God, to Thee*
> *Be endless honours done,*
> *The undivided Three,*
> *And the mysterious One.*
> *Where reason fails, with all her powers,*
> *There faith prevails and love adores.*
> *Isaac Watts*

The God-man is the biggest stumbling block for Muslims, but for Bible believers it is one of the glorious mysteries of the Christian faith. The Trinity is a doctrine that Muslims (or anyone else) must come to believe in by acceptance of Bible revelation, not by rational speculation *(Acts 9.20-22; Matthew 16.15-17)*. It is above reason, but not contrary to it. No one can fully do justice to the greatness of God. Language is unable to express the depths of this mystery. The Church Fathers used a triangle to explain the Trinity, but they would not illustrate the Trinity on a vertical surface, because that would denote seniority. Instead, they would paint it on a ceiling or on a horizontal surface to show the absolute and perfect equality in the Godhead. The Puritans illustrated it by reference to the sun, its beams, and its heat. A simple plant or flower has also served as a picture, having three parts: root, stem and flower – and yet it is one. But all depictions are inadequate. As believers we know God, we have a personal relationship with Him; and yet He still remains gloriously mysterious in His unfathomable triune nature.

Trinity means literally 'three-in-one', a mystery revealed in Scripture *(Genesis 1.26; 3.22; 11.7; 16.7-13; 18.1-21; 19.1-28; Judges 13; Psalm 2.6-12; 45.6-7; Isaiah 6.8; 48.12-16; 63.7-10; Matthew 3.16-17; 28.19; John 14.16; 1 Corinthians 12.4-6; 2 Corinthians 13.14; Hebrews 9.14; 1 Peter 1.2; 1 John 5.7-8)*. We bow in adoration where our limited minds cannot fully understand. We know that without the doctrine of the Trinity, there would be no salvation, because only the God-man, Christ, could offer a sufficient sacrifice to atone for the sins of men and women. This is truly the great difference between Islam and Christianity.

3. The Person of the Lord Jesus Christ: Approved but Misunderstood

ALTHOUGH the Qur'an emphatically denies the deity of the Lord Jesus Christ and curses all who confess Him as Lord *(Surah 9.30; cf. 5.72)*, significantly it does present Christ as a unique person *(Surah 3.52; 5.19)*. The Qur'an has many things to say about the Lord Jesus. It attributes titles to Christ by which no other is described, to the point that many Muslims believe that they honour Christ more than Christians do!

- The Lord Jesus is considered to be one of the major prophets of Islam – even though Muslims are taught not to make distinctions between them *(Surah 2.130, 285; 3.78)*. His name appears alongside Abraham's with all the great prophets *(Surah 6.84)*.
- He is mentioned twenty-five times in the Qur'an, and allusions to Him occur in ninety-three verses. Surprisingly, He is mentioned more often than Muhammad! At the same time we have to be

cautious. One can justifiably conclude that the *Isa* (Jesus) of the Qur'an is a different Lord Jesus from that of the Bible.

• The Qur'an also denies the divine sonship of Christ *(Surah 4.171)*.

• The Qur'an speaks about His miracles, some performed from His childhood onwards *(Surah 5.110)*, but never quotes or refers to His biblical teaching or prophecies. The One who spoke and taught like no other *(John 7.46)* is almost completely silent in the Qur'an. It is worth noting that while the Qur'an dwells at some length on Christ's miraculous birth, it does not mention Muhammad's birth at all.

Here are some of the most notable characteristics by which the Lord Jesus Christ is described in the Qur'an – characteristics peculiar to God alone!

• He was born to be a 'sign' for all men, and an example for the children of Israel *(Surah 3.49; 21.91; 43.59; cf. Isaiah 7.14)*. This is not said of any other prophet. Muslims will question why we make so much of the Lord Jesus' birth from a virgin, because Adam had neither *father* nor *mother*, they argue. The difference is important: Adam was *created* not *born*, while Christ was born, though without a father, because He already existed, and entered into human form. His birth is without parallel, it is utterly unique.

• He is called the 'Holy Child' and blessed of God *(Surah 19.19-20, 30)*, who is born of a virgin. Significantly, His father is never mentioned (which is especially strange in an Arab culture, where paternity is paramount), and, in fact, He is often referred to as the 'son of Mary' *(Surah 5.75, 78, 110, 112; 4.46, 171; 61.6)*, emphasising His virginal conception for those with eyes to see and ears to hear.

• In the Qur'an, Jesus Christ is called Muhammad's 'Lord' *(Surah 2.91)*.

• He is the only sinless prophet *(Surah 19.19, 31-32; cf. Hebrews*

7.26). Whilst every other prophet is sinful and seeks forgiveness before God, the Lord Jesus never does. No sin of any kind is ascribed to Him. He was above reproach and pure. He was holy, blameless, undefiled, free from evil, and without any transgression, in stark contrast to the rest of mankind (prophets and messengers included). Muhammad confessed on several occasions that he was a sinner *(Surah 18.110; 48.2),* and Allah told Muhammad to repent of his sins *(Surah 40.55).* The Bible teaches that a sinless sacrifice was essential for the salvation of men and women.

- He is called *Kalimatu'Allah* (the 'Word of God', *Surah 3.39; 4.171).* This is His most popular title in the Qur'an, and a title which reflects *John 1.1-18.* God and His Word must certainly be one and the same.
- He is referred to as *Ruah* (spirit) or *Ruhun min Allah* (Spirit of God – *Surah 4.171; cf. 3.45).* If the Lord Jesus is the *Word* and the *Spirit* of Allah, what would remain of Allah if his Spirit and Word were ever removed from him? So Christ, being the Word of God, and His Spirit must necessarily be God also.
- He is highly praised and portrayed as 'great and illustrious in this world and the next' *(Surah 3.46; 33.69),* which is not said of any other prophet. The Bible tells us that Christ, the Son of God, has been given the highest place, above men and angels *(Psalm 110.1; Hebrews 1.1-13).*
- He is the only one referred to as the Messiah *(Al-Masih,* the Anointed One) eleven times *(Surah 3.45; 4.157, 171-172; 9.31,* amongst others) – even though Muhammad gives no idea what this actually means. The Qur'an never explains this and in fact says that He was no more than a prophet *(Surah 4.171).*
- He is also the *Word* and the *Speech of Truth (Surah 19.34-35).*
- He is a *Mercy from Allah (Surah 19.21).*
- He has power to create *(Surah 5.113),* and power to raise the dead *(Surah 3.49; 5.113).* The Lord Jesus in the Qur'an healed

the sick, cleansed the lepers, gave sight to the blind, raised the dead to life, and brought a table furnished with food from Heaven *(Surah 5.110, 116)*. Muslims still believe today in the healing power of Christ and in His power to do miracles. This is why some Muslims will ask Christians to pray for them.

- He is alive and in Heaven *(Surah 3.55)*. Muslims believe that Christ is still alive (having never been crucified but taken up to Heaven before the cross). Until He dies (He never can or will, *Revelation 1.18*), there can be no question of a successor. So Muhammad cannot be His successor.

It is worth noting that five times a day in prayer every Muslim prays, 'Peace be upon Muhammad'. They pray that God will grant him (ie: Muhammad) entry into Heaven. A man can give only what he already has. If Muhammad has no place in Heaven, or 'peace', to start with, how can he possibly give it to others? If the leader of Islam himself does not know where he is going, what about his followers? By contrast, Christians do not need to pray for the Lord Jesus, 'Peace be upon Him', because He is the Lord of all and a member of the Triune Godhead with the divine power to bring anything to pass. He is the Prince of Peace *(Isaiah 9.6)*, the peace-giver *(John 14.27; Colossians 1.20)*, 'For in him dwelleth all the fulness of the Godhead bodily' *(Colossians 2.9)*. Christ is our 'peace' *(Ephesians 2.14)* and He gives us true spiritual peace.

4. The Title 'Son of God' – The Great Confusion

(Surah 19.35, 91-93; cf. 17.112; 43.59)

THIS is the most offensive title conceivable to Muslims for one simple reason: it is misunderstood. We need to explain to them that our belief in Jesus as the Son of God is not that of a son in a physical or biological sense. Mary was not God's wife! To think or to suggest that is offensive to us also. Let them know that to say or to think such a thing is also blasphemous to us. The Qur'an agrees that the Lord Jesus was born of a virgin, Allah bringing this about without using the normal biological means. It was a miracle in the Qur'an and the Bible that had never happened before and will never happen again. Even so, the Lord Jesus is still thought to be just a mere man in the Qur'an and in Islam, although a great one.

However, 'Son of God' is not just His title; it is both His name and His nature. The Father said in *Matthew 3.17*, 'This is my beloved

Son.' The Lord Jesus didn't *become* the Son of God when He was born on earth; He has always *been* the Son of God from all eternity. Muslims ask: 'How could God have a son?' In *Proverbs 30.4* the question is asked: 'Who hath ascended up into heaven, or descended? who hath gathered the wind in his fists? who hath bound the waters in a garment? who hath established all the ends of the earth? what is his name, and what is his son's name, if thou canst tell?' By an eternal decree, in eternity past, present and future, God declared that He has anointed His Son as King *(Psalm 2.6-12; cf. Acts 13.33; Hebrews 1.5)*. Being God's Son does not denote a literal birth, but the closest relationship. For example, two of the Lord's disciples (John and James) are referred to as 'sons of thunder', but no one would interpret this literally, or think that 'thunder' therefore had a wife! Outside the Bible one finds a fellow-citizen referred to as a 'son of the country', or a traveller as a 'son of the road', or a student as a 'son of the school'. The Qur'an itself is called *Umm-al-kitab* (the 'Mother of all books'), but no one thinks it gave birth literally to all other books. Similarly, God does not have a son in a biological sense.

The sonship of Christ is an unfathomable eternal relationship within the Triune Godhead. God the Father eternally 'begets' God the Son *(John 1.18)*, and the two relate to one another in loving union and communion as Father and Son, but in a far higher spiritual sphere. To add to an already incomprehensible mystery, God the Son then took to Himself a human body in the incarnation, becoming the God-man having both a divine and human nature, inseparably joined together in one Person.

The term 'Son' is used partly to help our limited human minds to understand that Christ came from God, although it is far deeper than that. His relation as *Son* means that He has an eternal and unique relationship with God as the Second Person of the Trinity. 'Son' is clearly not used to mean a biological relationship or birth by procreation. Here are some scriptural references showing the Lord Jesus is to be called the 'Son of God'.

- He is the 'only begotten Son, which is in the bosom of the Father, he hath declared him' *(John 1.18)*.
- The Son was with God in the beginning and is God, and He is the image of His Father *(John 1.1; 14.9; Colossians 1.15)*.
- God calls Him 'Son' and He calls God 'Father'. He knows the Father and knows His will as the 'beloved Son' *(Matthew 11.25-27; John 8.28-29; Hebrews 1.5)*.
- The *Gospel of Mark* commences with the clear statement: 'The beginning of the gospel of Jesus Christ, the Son of God.'
- The angel Gabriel announced the Lord Jesus before His conception as the Son of God *(Luke 1.32, 35)*.
- The devil knew well that He claimed to be the 'Son of God' *(Matthew 4.3, 6)*, and the demons too *(Mark 3.11)*.
- Peter made his great declaration of Christ's sonship, which the Lord accepted and endorsed *(Matthew 16.16-17)*.
- Following Pentecost, the sermons of the apostles often referred to Christ's sonship *(Acts 3.13, 26; 4.27; 8.37; 9.20; 13.33)*.
- Throughout the New Testament, He is identified as the Son of God (eg: *Romans 1.3-4; 1 Corinthians 1.9; Galatians 4.4; Ephesians 4.13; Colossians 1.13; Hebrews 1.2; 1 John 1.3)*.
- John the Baptist identified Him as the Son of God *(John 1.34; 3.34-36)*.
- His disciples identified Him as God *(John 1.1, 18; 20.28, 31; Philippians 2.5-11; Colossians 2.9)*.
- The Bible declares Christ, the Messiah, to be 'the mighty God' *(Isaiah 9.6)*, and 'the great God and our Saviour' *(Titus 2.13)*.
- In the beginning was the Word: the Lord Jesus Christ, God the Creator made flesh *(John 1.1-3, 14, 18; Colossians 1.16-17; Hebrews 1.1-3, 8-12; 1 John 1.1-3; 5.20)*.
- Old Testament prophets before Christ's coming to this earth believed that He would be God Himself *(Psalm 2.10-12; 45.6-7,* quoted in *Hebrews 1.8-9; Psalm 110.1,* quoted by Christ in *Matthew 22.42-45; Isaiah 6.1-3, 9-10; cf. John 12.41; Isaiah*

7.14; 9.6-7; 52.13-53.12; Jeremiah 23.5-6; 33.15; Daniel 7.13-14;
9.24-27).

- The day is coming when 'at the name of Jesus every knee should
  bow, of things in heaven, and things in earth, and things under
  the earth; and...every tongue should confess that Jesus
  Christ is Lord, to the glory of God the Father' *(Philippians
  2.10-11)*.

Muslims love to tell Christians that the Lord Jesus never said He
was God or the Son of God. They even say that there is not a single
verse about it in the whole Bible. If this were true, why did the Jews
seek to stone Him for blasphemy? *(John 8.58-59; 10.30-39)*. The
people in Christ's time understood very well that He made Himself
equal to God. Why did He say, 'All power is given unto me in heaven
and in earth'? *(Matthew 28.18)*. This would make no sense if He
were not God.

Is it true that the Lord Jesus never said that He was God or the
Son of God? Consider these passages:

- The Lord Jesus referred to Himself both directly and indirectly
  as the 'Son of God' throughout the Gospels (eg: *Matthew 11.25-
  27; John 3.16-18*); and He spoke unambiguously of His sonship
  (John 5.22-23; 8.35-36; 9.35-38; 10.30-33; 14.13; 17.1-3).
- He identified Himself as God revealed in the flesh *(John 8.56-59)*.
- The Jews claimed He blasphemously said He was the Son of God
  (Mark 14.61-64; John 19.7). They understood His claim correctly.
  Christ openly said that He was the Son of God.
- Why was He crucified? Because He made himself equal with
  God *(John 5.17-18; 10.30, 33; 14.1)*. The Jews knew undoubt-
  edly what Christ meant, and that He claimed to be fully God and
  fully man.
- He was worshipped as divine on earth, and never prevented
  anyone from doing so, even though this is the exclusive preroga-
  tive of God alone (eg: *Matthew 14.33; John 20.28-29; cf.* Paul and
  Barnabas at Lystra, *Acts 14.11-18)*.

- The angels worship Him *(Hebrews 1.6)*, and He could command legions of angels *(Matthew 26.53)*. He exercised total control over the demonic realm (eg: *Matthew 9.32-34; Mark 3.11-12; Luke 8.26ff)*.
- The wise men worshipped Him while He was still a child *(Matthew 2.11)*.
- A poor leper worshipped Him *(Matthew 8.2)*, to which He responded with a divine miracle of healing.
- He alone could give rest to the soul, another divine prerogative *(Matthew 11.28-30)*.
- He assumed authority to forgive sin, and who but God can forgive sin? *(Matthew 9.2-8)*. His enemies called it blasphemy.
- No mere man can see God and live, but Christ testified that He had seen the Father, and that He was with the Father *(John 3.13; 6.46)*, and that whoever had seen Him had seen the Father, for He is one with the Father *(John 10.30; 14.9-13)*.
- The Lord's favourite title for Himself which He habitually used was 'Son of man'. Properly understood it is a divine title for the incarnate Son that speaks of divine authority *(Luke 6.5; 19.10)*, and is effectively equivalent to 'Son of God'. See *Matthew 26.63-66* where the Jews condemned Him as worthy of death for blasphemy. The Old Testament background to this title is *Daniel 7.13-14*, where it is clearly a divine title indicating a divine relationship with God. The Lord is referring to this in *Matthew 26.64*.
- His great 'I am' sayings clearly identified Him as the only and true God of the Old and New Testaments *(Exodus 3.15; cf. John 6.35; 8.12; 10.9, 11; 11.25; 14.6; 15.1)*.

Consider also the things He did of His own will and power that only God could do:

- He did great miracles, such as feeding thousands on two separate occasions *(Matthew 14.14-21; 15.32-38)*, and turning water into wine *(John 2.1-11)*.

- He exercised absolute mastery over the forces of nature: He stilled a storm, and He walked on the sea *(Matthew 14.24-33; Mark 4.35-41).*
- He healed multitudes, many of whom had hopeless and irreversible illnesses *(Matthew 4.23-25; John 9.1-7).*
- He raised the dead *(Mark 5.41-42; Luke 7.11-15; John 11.43-44).*

The Son of God is no less than God. His deity is vital for anyone to understand the Godhead, the Trinity and salvation.

5. Christ's Death on the Cross: Fact or Fiction?

THE CRUCIFIXION of Christ is a central issue of dispute between Christianity and Islam. No one before Muhammad had denied the death of Christ on the cross. Islam has always been opposed to the atoning work of the Lord Jesus Christ on the cross of Calvary, through the centuries and throughout the world. Point by point Islam denies the fundamentals of Christianity, but especially the cross, the very centre of our faith. Islam insists: 'But they [the Jews] killed him not, nor crucified him, but so it was made to appear to them' *(Surah 4.157)*.

It is reported by tradition that Muhammad broke everything brought to his house with a cross upon it. Muslims see the cross as a defeat, when actually the death of Christ and His resurrection together was the greatest victory in all the history of this universe. Christ conquered death, sin and the devil on behalf of those who repent and trust in His precious blood. Any doctrine of substitutionary atonement is absent from Islamic belief: 'No bearer of burdens will bear the burden of another' *(Surah 53.38; 17.15; 39.7)*.

How do we deal with the Islamic insistence that the Lord Jesus did not die on the cross? We should point to Old Testament passages which predicted the sufferings of the Messiah, and also the passages in the New Testament where the Lord Jesus *Himself* predicted His own death. Then we point to the evidence of the Lord's death, particularly the testimony of the Gospels.

Some Muslims believe that the Lord Jesus was tortured on the cross, but that He did not die there. However, oddly, there *are* two main passages in the Qur'an *(Surah 3.55; 4.157-158)* which make an allusion to Christ's death, and yet Muslims persist in denying such a possibility. The Qur'an states: 'but it was made to appear to them...' *(Surah 4.157)*. These words suggest a 'swap or replacement theory'. In other words, the disciples were simply victims of an illusion. It was all a hoax of the early church, so Muslims say. The Lord was quickly taken up to Heaven before His crucifixion, and Judas (or Simon of Cyrene) died on the cross instead of Him. In other words, it was not the Lord Jesus dying for men, but a man dying (on the cross) for the Lord Jesus Christ. This is a direct denial of Christ's atonement. The question is, why should God lift up Christ into Heaven and put someone else on the cross?

Why did the cross become a symbol if He had not died on it? There are more evidences of His death than there are for Muhammad's revelations. The events around Calvary were witnessed by so many. And consider the following:

- His crucifixion was foretold *(Psalm 22; Isaiah 53; Zechariah 12.10)*.
- The records of Roman and Jewish history leave no doubt about Christ's death, including the Jewish historian Flavius Josephus, the Roman historian Cornelius Tacitus (first century AD), and Lucian the Greek (second century AD).

- On five occasions He said that He was going to die *(Matthew 12.39-40; 16.21; 17.22-23; 20.18-19; 26.1-2 and parallels)*. Two of these passages *(Matthew 20.18-19; 26.1-2)* explicitly mention crucifixion. While He could have avoided the cross, He was clearly determined to go there.

- He was betrayed to *death* by Judas, a friend, as prophesied *(Psalm 41.9; 55.12-14, 20-21; Zechariah 11.12-13; Matthew 26.3-4, 14-16; Luke 22.48)*.

- He was arrested in Gethsemane by a band of soldiers to go to trial for His life *(John 18.3)*.

- The high priest prophesied that one should *die* for the people *(John 18.14)*.

- At Christ's death, the curtain in the Temple separating the most holy place was torn in two, to symbolise the free access of men to God through His death alone *(Matthew 27.51)*.

- It is plainly recorded that 'when Jesus therefore had received the vinegar, he said, It is finished: and he bowed his head, and gave up the ghost' *(John 19.30)*.

- Mary, His mother, was at the cross, and a mother would surely not mistake someone else for her son, especially as she weeps for Him in His dying agonies *(John 19.25-27)*.

- Some of His followers were witnesses of His crucifixion *(John 19.25-27)*.

- Pilate had to be sure that He had *died* before he gave permission to have His body removed from the cross and then *buried* in a rich man's sepulchre (as it had been prophesied seven hundred years before, *Isaiah 53.9; Mark 15.43-45*).

- Knowing He was dead but fearful the disciples might steal His body, the Jews asked Pilate for a guard for the tomb, saying: 'Sir, we remember that that deceiver said, *while he was yet alive*, After three days I will rise again' *(Matthew 27.63)*.

- The common soldiers knew He was dead and the Jews demanded He be dead before sunset *(John 19.30-37)*.

- If Christ's *death* was just a myth, why did all His apostles, with the exception of John, probably die as martyrs for their beliefs? A man may give his life for a noble cause, but no one would sacrifice his life *knowingly* for a lie or a fairy tale.
- The early church went about everywhere proclaiming His *death* and resurrection. 'Him, being delivered by the determinate counsel and foreknowledge of God, ye have taken, and by wicked hands have crucified and slain: whom God hath raised up, having loosed the pains of death: because it was not possible that he should be holden of it' *(Acts 2.23-24)*.

Indeed, on that day for six whole hours, Christ was truly on the cross, where He truly died. Above all that, how can a great and holy God, Who hates lying, deceive or mislead people by crucifying another man in Christ's stead? It is impossible for Him to make use of a lie. That goes against His very nature *(Titus 1.2)*.

The Cross is a shame in one sense, but at the same time it is a great victory. 'But God forbid that I should glory, save in the cross of our Lord Jesus Christ' *(Galatians 6.14)*. Through the Cross God shows not only His hatred of sin, but also His great love towards sinners. There is no other way to Heaven but through the Cross of Christ, which is why He endured it. His crucifixion exposes our evil and wicked nature, and through it are displayed God's love, grace, wisdom, power and mercy.

Even though there is in the Qur'an a blunt denial of Christ's death, there are other verses which seem to say that the Lord was killed *(Surah 4.157-158; 3.55; 5.117)*. 'And peace is on me the day I was born and the day I will die and the day I am raised alive. That is Jesus, the son of Mary – the word of truth' *(Surah 19.34)*. Though Islam denies the crucifixion of the Lord, how could these verses speak about the resurrection of someone who is not dead?

Christ 'will destroy the Evil one and will live on the earth for forty years and then will die' *(Abu Dawood, 37.4310, narrated by*

Abu Huraira). By tradition (not in the Qur'an) Muslims believe that Christ will come again, and that He will die and be buried near Muhammad, having married and sired children, and having slaughtered all Christians who do not convert to Islam. He will then break every cross and reign over all Muslims (which contradicts *Surah 5.69*, which says the opposite). Christ then is the only prophet in Islam who will play a paramount role in the end times and in the world to come. Christ according to the Scriptures is coming back not to die again but to fulfil what He has promised: 'Let not your heart be troubled: ye believe in God, believe also in me. In my Father's house are many mansions: if it were not so, I would have told you. I go to prepare a place for you. And if I go and prepare a place for you, I will come again, and receive you unto myself; that where I am, there ye may be also' *(John 14.1-3)*.

The Bible says: 'Moreover, brethren, I declare unto you the gospel which I preached unto you, which also ye have received, and wherein ye stand; by which also ye are saved, if ye keep in memory what I preached unto you, unless ye have believed in vain. For I delivered unto you first of all that which I also received, how that Christ died for our sins according to the scriptures; and that he was buried, and that he rose again the third day according to the scriptures' *(1 Corinthians 15.1-4; cf. 1 Peter 3.18)*.

6. The Scriptures —
The Great Misconception

(Surah 5.47; 10.94-95; 48.23)

THE QUR'AN IS believed by Muslims to have been dictated word by word in beautiful Arabic to Muhammad by the angel Gabriel. On the other hand, the Bible was written by men infallibly inspired by God to write by the Holy Spirit *(2 Peter 1.19-21)*. It is divine and God-given. The Holy Spirit is the Author of the Bible. Yet this divine book is also a human book, for the Holy Spirit used and guided the differing personalities and abilities of each penman of Holy Scripture to write exactly what He wanted written. Can two books, supposedly from the same God, be so contradictory? They surely cannot be from the same God to be so much in conflict. Is the angel Gabriel in the Qur'an the same as the one in the Bible? Clearly not! How can we have a situation where every prophet gives the same message except one, namely Muhammad? In the great chain of Old Testament prophets, none of them contradicted their predecessors, and there are endless prophecies about Christ in the Old Testament. Christ spoke by His own authority, while Muhammad spoke by the authority of a supposed angel. If the same Allah gave both revelations, it is only logical that their ministries and messages would not contradict each other.

The fact that the authentic Qur'an can only be in Arabic (considered to be the language of Heaven) and cannot be translated (only 'interpreted') surely shows that it is not a revelation to all mankind. In fact, we must presume that it was not intended for all Muslims, because most of them cannot read Arabic. Even among Arabs the illiteracy rate is still high. The universal translatability of the Bible into any and every language makes it truly the people's Book. When translated into any language it retains its power to convict, to convert, to guide, and to guard, because it is given by the Spirit. (Yet Muslims cannot recognise the converting power of the Spirit through the Word, as they deny personal salvation.)

Muslims will tell you that they know what the Qur'an says, but that is not always true. It is just like many nominal Christians who may have a Bible on their shelves, but have never read it. Christians are officially called in the Qur'an *Ahl-Alkitab* (People of the Book) some forty times, and *Ahl-Linjil* (People of the Gospel). Muslims are supposed to go and ask the Christians about things they do not understand in reading their own Qur'an *(Surah 2.130, 136; 16.93; 21.7)*. We could say to Muslims: 'If you really believe in Adam, Noah, Abraham, Moses, David, Solomon, etc, you should also believe in Christ' *(cf. Galatians 3.29)*.

The Qur'an declares that the Bible, both Old and New Testaments, is from God *(Surah 3.3; 5.46, 66; 7.145)*. The Bible is called 'the Book' more than twenty times; 'the Proof'; '*Al-Dhikr*' (meaning 'remembrance'); 'a light, an admonition and a guide to man' for those who have the heart to respond *(Surah 3.3, 65; 5.46-47, 66, 68)*; 'sight for the people' *(Surah 28.43)*; 'an explanation of all things and a decision for all matters' *(Surah 6.91, 154)*. It is written in the Qur'an that no one can change the Word of God *(Surah 6.34, 115; 35.43; 48.23)*.

Muslims will not, however, be inclined to listen to our use of the Bible, as they believe that the Bible we now possess is not the same as it was in the time of Muhammad. Many of them believe that the Bible has been changed, and certain truths have been eliminated and others have been added. This misinformation has been passed down through the centuries and this is the universal teaching of Islam. The first Muslim attack regarding the authenticity of the Bible came in the eleventh century, by which time it had spread to many nations, and been translated into several languages. The Jews had many sinful failures for which the Lord blamed them, but He never accused them of corrupting or changing the Scriptures. For all their wrong deeds and acts, they never changed the Word of God. They have provided a custodian care to God's Word. It is just out of the question that Christians and Jews sat down together to agree to change certain parts of the Scripture, as Muslims claim. They were notoriously hostile to one another in many ways. The Bible we have today is exactly the same Bible that people were reading before the death of Muhammad in AD 632. Misinterpretation of the text is not to be confused with corruption of the text *(Surah 2.75)*. It is simply impossible for a book so well-circulated in the civilised world, both before and after the birth of Islam, to be corrupted without provoking a general outcry. There is an awesome warning for people who dare to change the Word of God *(Deuteronomy 4.2; 12.32; Proverbs 30.5-6; Revelation 22.18-19)*. So would Christians (or Jews) dare do such a thing? Is God so weak that He cannot protect His living Word? Invite Muslims to read the Bible: there is obvious harmony and unity in it.

There is a difference between making an accusation and providing evidence for it. We must gently challenge them to demonstrate exactly when, by whom, where, and why the Bible was corrupted, as well as which parts of it. Was it before or after the arrival of the Qur'an in the seventh century? What are the historical sources and the textual evidence for this allegation? Who is thought to have made the changes? As one seeks answers, it becomes clear that the accusations of Islam are not connected with any known time or place. They are unfounded and mythical.

Facts about the Qur'an

If Muslims judged the Qur'an using the same criteria that they use to judge the Bible, they would quickly be disenchanted.

- The manuscripts of the Bible are very much older than the Qur'an.
- Nine important language versions of the Bible were available before the Qur'an: Hebrew, Aramaic, the Septuagint, Syriac (known as the Peshitto), Coptic (Upper Egypt), Bohairic or Ramphitic (Lower Egypt), Gu'iz (Abyssinian Empire), Georgian (Caucasus) and Latin (Vulgate).
- Many Muslims have never read or even touched a Qur'an. All they know is what the *imam* (leader of the mosque) says. They depend on his knowledge. In most cases, the imam reads a verse from the Qur'an, and then gives his 'interpretation' of the verse in the congregation's own language. Is that not in effect a translation?
- Is there a Muslim anywhere who has the original copy of the Qur'an? The answer is no. There never was one, because in the beginning it was written on palm leaves, camel ribs and shoulder blades, flat stones, wooden boards, etc. Most of the text came from the memory of the reciters, the original companions of the prophet (*Qur'an* means to read or to recite). However, we know human memory is far from infallible.
- Since the Qur'an has itself affirmed that the Bible is the Word of God, how can Muslims consider it has been changed or corrupted?
- Muslims believe that the Qur'an fulfilled and confirmed the Bible, so that the focus is now on the Qur'an and not on the Bible. However, they present totally contradictory messages of

God and how to know Him. The Qur'an declares that the Bible was given by God to the prophets and to the Lord Jesus *(Surah 2.50; 3.3; 5.50; 6.91; 11.20; 19.31; 21.27; 25.37; 32.23; 37.117; 40.56; 57.27).*

- Even with the textual variants and other changes alleged by Muslims, the main message of salvation in Christ is still crystal clear.

- Muslims are commanded in numerous passages to read and learn from the Bible and not to argue with the People of the Book. 'If thou wert in doubt as to what we have revealed unto thee, then ask those who have been reading the Book from before thee' *(Surah 10.94; cf. 3.3, 84; 5.46).*

- The Qur'an shows that before the birth of Islam the Bible was uncorrupted, and bears witness to the inerrancy of the Bible *(Surah 15.9; 21.7, 48, 105; 18.27).* Before the birth of Islam, the Bible had already enjoyed five centuries of deep historical and theological foundations.

- God originally inspired His Word in Hebrew (Old Testament) and Greek (New Testament), meaning it to be translated into all languages, for it still remains the Word of God. The Qur'an is considered by Muslims to be effectively untranslatable. Christians can study the Bible, but non-Arabic speaking Muslims can never really look deeply into the Qur'an. It is a closed book to them, despite every aspect of their lives being governed by it.

- The Qur'an states: 'Recite [O Muhammad], what has been revealed to you of the Book and establish prayer. Indeed, prayer prohibits immorality and wrongdoing, and the remembrance of Allah is greater. And Allah knows that which you do. And do not argue with the People of the Scripture except in a way that is best, except for those who commit injustice among them...' *(Surah 29.45-46).*

7. Was Muhammad Foretold in the Bible?

(*Deuteronomy 18.15-19; Song of Songs 5.16; John 14.16, 26; 16.7-14; Surah 7.157*)

TO UPHOLD THE VALIDITY of Muhammad's teaching, Muslims try to use every possible argument to convince others (especially Christians) that Muhammad is mentioned in the Bible. They will argue for example that the word 'Hallelujah' in the Bible actually means 'Praise to Allah'; 'Amen' means 'Ahmend', that is to say, Muhammad! If it is not there, they insist that the Bible must have been corrupted and can no longer be trusted. What is more, the phrase 'most sweet' in the *Song of Songs 5.16* is regarded as another reference to Muhammad – the Hebrew *machamaddim* is said to be *machamad* or Muhammad in Aramaic! This seems unlikely in the extreme.

Real prophets and apostles were called directly by God, equipped to do mighty deeds, and sent to carry out their given tasks. Muslims are absolutely certain that Muhammad's name and coming were predicted in the Bible, but obscured by deliberate corruption of the text by Christians *(Surah 61.6)*. However, the truth is that in spite of these claims, Muhammad is not mentioned anywhere in the Bible.

Deuteronomy 18.15-19 is a key text on which they base their argument. Moses said that God would raise up another 'Prophet' like Moses from among the Jews. Moses was speaking to the tribes of Israel as he was about to leave this world. The Prophet would be a Jew and, of course, Christ was a Jew. As far as we know Muhammad was not a Jew. He was from Arabia, and the Arabs are not one of the twelve tribes of Israel. He is therefore ruled out from the start as a possible fulfilment of this text. Peter, in one of the very first sermons preached after the New Testament Church was born, tells us that this promised Prophet was Christ *(Acts 3.22-23; cf. 7.37)*. Christ was to be born in Bethlehem *(Micah 5.2)*. That was not the case for Muhammad, who was born in Mecca in Arabia, not Bethlehem.

'From the midst of thee, of thy brethren' *(Deuteronomy 18.15)* the future 'Prophet' would come, that is from the twelve tribes of Israel, descended from the patriarch Jacob. The term 'brethren' could not possibly refer to the Ishmaelites (who Muslims say descended from Abraham's *favourite* son, *Ishmael*, the ancestor of all Arabs, or so they claim). The blessing God promised would come from Isaac not Ishmael.

Moses said 'like unto me', therefore, the promised Prophet must be like Moses, who was raised up for the deliverance of his people and who performed many miracles. Muhammad never performed such wonderful and mighty deeds; in fact, he admitted he never performed any miracles *at all (Surah 6.50; 29.50)*.

God spoke face-to-face with Moses, which was never the case for Muhammad *(Surah 42.52-53)*. No wonder the Jews refused to recognise Muhammad as a prophet.

As was the case with Christ, Moses was a *mediator* between God and the people *(Deuteronomy 18.16)*. A covenant was made through Moses' mediation at Mount Sinai. Muhammad never acted as a mediator, only as a claimed mouthpiece for Allah.

The New Testament alludes to this prophecy when speaking of the Lord Jesus Christ *(Luke 24.19, 27; John 1.45; Acts 3.22-23; Hebrews 3.1-6)*.

Stephen, the first Christian martyr, gave testimony before the Sanhedrin, that the Lord Jesus was indeed the long-awaited prophet foretold by Moses *(Acts 7.37)*.

There are many other similarities between Moses and the Lord Jesus which Muhammad did not share. In addition to working miracles and being mediators, both Moses and Christ experienced many significant similarities, such as: their infant lives were endangered, they were called out of Egypt, and they suffered humiliation and rejection by their own people. Muhammad's career was altogether different.

All Muslims recognise Moses as a great prophet and they believe in his writings and message. They do not know that Christ said: 'For had ye believed Moses, ye would have believed me: for he wrote of me. But if ye believe not his writings, how shall ye believe my words?' *(John 5.46-47)*.

The prophecy of *Deuteronomy 18* was fulfilled unmistakably in Jesus Christ centuries before the birth of Muhammad. It does not fit Muhammad, who spoke on behalf of Allah, and not on behalf of the Almighty God of the Bible.

In summary, Moses was a great and good man (as *Numbers 12.3* and *Deuteronomy 34.10* bear witness), but Jesus Christ the God-man is infinitely greater. Christ is the King of kings and Lord of lords; greater than Abraham, Moses, David, Solomon, indeed greater than all the prophets put together. He is Lord and Saviour. He is the fulfilment of all the prophets, being the final and greatest prophet from God, His very Son, in Whom is the forgiveness of sin *(Acts 10.43; Hebrews 1.1-3)*.

The prophets and apostles have all finished their work and are now deceased, but Christ remains for ever the same in all His offices *(Hebrews 13.8)*. The Lord Jesus provides a better hope than Moses

(Hebrews 3.1-6; 8.6). 'They saw no man, save Jesus only' *(Matthew 17.8)* is the inspired comment after Moses and Elijah vanished, leaving only the transfigured Christ on the mount, alone in His transcendent glory as the Incarnate Son, the One Who fulfils all prophecy. Christ, unquestionably, was the promised Prophet to come *(John 6.14).*

Is Muhammad really the promised Comforter?

In the Qur'an we read: 'And when Jesus, the son of Mary, said, "O children of Israel, indeed I am the messenger of Allah to you confirming what came before me of the Torah and bringing good tidings of a messenger to come after me, whose name is Ahmad"' *(Surah 61.6).* But nowhere in the New Testament did the Lord Jesus utter such words.

Muslims strongly argue that the Greek word *parakletos* used of the Holy Spirit in *John 14.16, 26; 15.26; 16.7,* meaning 'Comforter, Helper or Advocate', should actually be *periklytos* 'the Exalted, Praised or Honoured one', which they say refers to Muhammad (his earthly name) and *Ahmad* (his heavenly name), and not to the Holy Spirit. This is the proof, they say, that the biblical text has been changed and is at variance with the Qur'an. If it had not been changed, we would have read that Muhammad is Christ's successor.

Thousands of Greek New Testament manuscripts have been preserved, many of them from long before the time of Islam and Muhammad. They may contain some textual variation and different spellings of words (though not affecting any Christian doctrine), but there is not a single one which has the spelling *periklytos.*

The Greek New Testament Scriptures emphatically do not support the Islamic proposal, and it is not credible to suggest that the fourth century manuscripts (and earlier) that we have were corrupted in anticipation of the arrival of Islam. But historically one of the characteristics of Islamic thought is that it is resistant to logic, reason and evidence; if the Qur'an says something, nothing can contradict it, whatever the evidence to the contrary.

John 16.7-11 reads: 'Nevertheless I tell you the truth; It is expedient for you that I go away: for if I go not away, the Comforter will not come unto you; but if I depart, I will send him unto you. And when he is come, he will reprove the world of sin, and of righteousness, and of judgment: of sin, because they believe not on me; of righteousness, because I go to my Father, and ye see me no more; of judgment, because the prince of this world is judged.'

Muslims, however, claim that the Lord said: 'After me I will send the Praised One [ie: Ahmad], and he shall guide you into all truth.' But we are told in *John's Gospel* that the Comforter or Helper proceeds from the Father and the Lord Jesus *(John 14.16; 15.26; 16.7)*. Although *John 14.16* is often quoted to claim that Christ refers to Muhammad, the question is: How can it be applied to the man who denied both Christ and His Father, when *John 16.14-15* says the Comforter will glorify Christ and by extension the Father?

The Comforter or Holy Spirit (in Islam, the angel Gabriel is the equivalent of the Holy Spirit) is described in Scripture in many ways that clearly show Muhammad is not in mind.

The Comforter is the Spirit of truth, not a man *(John 16.13)*. The Lord Jesus referred to the promised Holy Spirit as the 'Spirit of truth' *(John 14.17)*. The Bible and the Qur'an contradict each other, because the Comforter is not human as the Qur'an teaches, but Spirit.

As the Comforter was given to us by Christ and the Father, so He is equal to the Father and the Son *(John 14.23-26)*.

The Comforter came fifty days, not five hundred years, after the resurrection of Christ, for He was promised to come to the disciples soon after Christ's ascension *(Acts 1.4-5)*.

The Comforter will abide with believers *for ever (John 14.16)*. Muhammad has been dead for centuries.

The Comforter is the *Spirit* of truth whom the world cannot see.

He cannot be seen, because He is a spiritual being *(John 14.17)*. Muhammad was mere flesh and blood.

The Comforter is known by us and dwells *with* us and *in* us *(John 14.17)*. He will be received by those who will believe in Christ *(John 7.39)*. Muhammad does not dwell with and in us, and is not known to us, whilst the Spirit is. All who truly repent and believe in the Lord Jesus are indwelt by the promised Holy Spirit, and will receive new life *(Romans 8.9-11)*.

The Comforter will remind believers of the words of Christ, which means He knows everything *(John 14.26; 16.13-14)*. Muhammad was not all-knowing, and certainly did not know what the Bible in general and the New Testament in particular taught. He did not bring to the disciples' remembrance what the Lord taught. The Holy Spirit did that.

The Comforter will not speak of Himself, but will glorify Christ. The Holy Spirit did not speak about Himself (as Muhammad did) but only of Christ *(John 15.26; 16.13-14)*.

The Comforter will 'reprove the world of sin, and of righteousness, and of judgment' *(John 16.8)*. Muhammad never reproved the world of sin or brought anyone under deep conviction of their sin. Unless we see our lost state and depraved condition as sinners, we will never seek the Lord. The true Comforter is the Holy Spirit, not Muhammad.

The Comforter would reveal to Christ's disciples things to come, by guiding them into all truth and by bringing all things spoken by Christ to their remembrance, and by inspiring the apostles to write the New Testament *(John 14.26; 16.13)*.

So we have a strange situation when devout and intelligent Muslims believe the Comforter promised in *John 14-16* is Muhammad. None of the statements listed above make any sense when applied to Muhammad. Christ was obviously and undoubtedly referring to the Holy Spirit, not to a man.

The Holy Spirit should not be confused with the angel Gabriel or the Lord Jesus. He is the third Person of the Holy Trinity, and He is called God and Lord *(Acts 5.3-4; 1 Corinthians 2.10; 2 Corinthians 3.18; Hebrews 9.14).*

Questions About Muhammad

We should never rush to answer questions about Muhammad's status, just as we should never attack the person of Muhammad. It is always better to reply that our opinion about him does not matter and that our message is about the Gospel and about Christ. But we can also let the Word of God speak, as it gives the perfect answer. Speaking of Christ, the Word says: 'To him give all the prophets witness, that through his name whosoever believeth in him shall receive remission of sins' *(Acts 10.43).* It is easy to demonstrate that what Muslims nowadays claim the Bible says about Muhammad is actually based on the pseudo-Gospel of Barnabas, written in the fifteenth century by an Italian convert to Islam who wanted to reconcile the two religions. It is a book peppered with contradictions.

It may be noted that Muhammad never performed a miracle, nor uttered a word of prophecy. Even though Muslims say that Muhammad was just a normal man, in practice he is extolled and exalted as if he were some kind of deity. He is the role model for hundreds of millions of people, down to the tiniest detail.

However, it is extremely dangerous for a non-Muslim (or Muslim) to speak a word against Muhammad, in any way, in the Muslim world. It is bound to generate outraged anger and violence, and is punishable by death. Nevertheless, Muhammad never fitted the criteria required of a prophet set out in *Deuteronomy 13.1-5; 18.20-22.* By contrast, there are many, many prophecies concerning the coming of the one 'like unto Moses', which are all perfectly fulfilled in Jesus Christ, the God-man: Prophet, Priest and King.

8. Allah – Is He the Same as God?

ALLAH IS THE PERSONAL name of God in Islam, but is he the same God that we find in the Bible? Do Christians and Muslims worship the same God? For Muslims, there is no doubt about it – there is only one God, so by definition this must be the deity of both Muslims and Christians *(Surah 29.46-48)*. Yet this is far from reality because 'Allah' of the Qur'an is not the same as the God of the Bible. There is a *massive* gulf between the two. The Islamic view of God is totally different from that of the Christian. Allah is not the Creator revealed in the Bible.

Before the founding of Islam, Allah was considered to be one god among many in pagan Arab religion, although the most prominent. Only after his first revelations did Muhammad say that every other god must be destroyed, and that Allah was to be the sole 'God' to be worshipped as the true God. The God of the Bible was never addressed as Allah, a title derived from a pagan, pre-Islamic deity worshipped in Mecca before Muhammad was born. The God of the

Bible has never been associated with idols. He remains utterly separate and distinct from pagan gods.

When we compare the Bible and the Qur'an we soon realise that they definitely do not speak about the same God or the same Jesus Christ. The God of the Bible came in the flesh, and He delights in personal fellowship with His children. The Lord Almighty said He would be a Father to us, and we would be His sons and daughters *(2 Corinthians 6.18)*. He is our Father, our Shepherd, our Lord, and our Saviour. Our God is Three-in-One. On the other hand, Allah is a remote unitary being who relates to no one *(Surah 4.171)*, and Muslims daily recite *Surah 112* which says 'God has no son'. Allah is never called in the Qur'an the 'God of Abraham, Isaac and Jacob', or the Father and Friend of believers.

The God of the Bible is a personal God, not a distant and unapproachable God, and He is consistent all the time.

The Qur'an does not use the word 'Father' to refer to God, and Muslims deny that God has or ever could have a Son. And yet the Son of God Himself, the Lord Jesus Christ, taught us to pray: 'Our Father...' *(Luke 11.1-4)*.

PART 3

HOW TO
HELP MUSLIMS

I N SEEKING TO REACH Muslims, we must bear in mind that they too are commanded to actively share their faith and invite others to the way of Allah. They are taught that their religion is the only true one. They are zealous, determined and imperturbable about their beliefs. To Muslims, any of the following are considered a great victory: (1) when a church building is purchased and transformed into a mosque; (2) when a Westerner is converted to Islam; and (3) when a Muslim marries a 'Christian' woman. These 'victories' are all taking place in our day.

But it is possible to reach Muslims for Christ. We have unprecedented opportunities to interact with Muslims from all around the world. There is a new paradigm – they come to us. So here are some approaches that Christians can use to engage Muslims in conversation. These are applicable to all to whom we witness everywhere, but more specifically to Muslims.

1. Know your Bible thoroughly

While we must have some understanding of Islamic beliefs, it is essential for us to know our Bible, and the doctrines and the theology of the Christian faith. It is crucial that we know our own message and its meaning. We must pray to the Lord to help us to grow in our understanding of God's Word and in our personal relationship with the Lord. Make clear to Muslims what it means to be a Christian. Establish the distinction between Western society and true Christianity (between nominal and true faith). It is not for us to present them with a lecture or two on Islam, as if we must provide them with a free course on their own religion! They are supposed to know it; we are not to instruct them on it. Our task is to prove that the Bible, even though it has been translated into hundreds of languages, has remained authentic, inerrant, trustworthy, and truthful.

2. Do not be intimidated

(1 Peter 3.14; cf. Psalm 56.11; 118.6-7; Matthew 10.28; Hebrews 13.6)

Do we really love their souls? Love banishes fear. 'There is no fear in love; but perfect love casteth out fear: because fear hath torment. He that feareth is not made perfect in love' *(1 John 4.18)*. Among the many impediments in witnessing to Muslims is the fear of man, because it can paralyse, and Satan uses it as a weapon. The fear of man blinds us and prevents us from witnessing; it must be overcome and replaced by the fear of the Lord, which is the beginning of knowledge *(Proverbs 1.7; 2 Corinthians 5.11)*.

We must trust in the presence and the power of the Holy Spirit to bring about conversions. It is not necessarily true that Muslims are harder to reach than other people. God does not have to deploy more power to convert a Muslim; and, after all, the heart of man is the same everywhere *(Jeremiah 17.9; Romans 3.10-23)*. No one is beyond the reach of God. Before the Lord opened our eyes and drew us and saved us, were we any more eager to listen than Muslims? Everyone is in need of the help of the Holy Spirit to see their rebellion and to ask for forgiveness. In fact, Muslims are normally far more 'religious' and more approachable than the average Westerner.

However, we do need to take account of the fact that they have been indoctrinated from birth *against* Christianity, and that their whole way of life from birth has been carefully crafted to oppose Christianity. But we should not be intimidated if the tone of their voice and words are aggressive, or if they give the impression they are *firm* in their belief.

3. Be affable and amiable

Truth must always be spoken in love *(Ephesians 4.15)*. The Gospel is not something, it is Someone. Live a life that shows the love of Christ in you. 'Let your light so shine before men, that they may see your good works, and glorify your Father which is in heaven' *(Matthew 5.16)*.

Show the love of Christ in sincerity, not merely out of duty. Be open-hearted in expressing the Faith to all sinners, but especially Muslims, who may feel rejected by Westerners. Love overcomes hatred, distrust and suspicion. It is no surprise that this is the second greatest commandment *(Mark 12.31)*. Love souls and have a passion for souls.

Be caring and helpful whenever and wherever possible, and not just at prearranged times *(Galatians 6.9)*.

Our task is to win the person, not the argument. There is no benefit in winning the argument and losing the soul. In discussion with Muslims, remember Paul's advice to Timothy: 'Charging them before the Lord that they strive not about words to no profit, but to the subverting of the hearers' *(2 Timothy 2.14)*. We are not seeking useless confrontations. Apologetics without the Gospel are useless. If a Muslim family are your neighbours, visit them and speak with them. If there is a Muslim in your place of work or study, build a relationship so that you may be a better witness. Deeds are more important than words for Muslims. Love them and take each opportunity as it arises.

Always be fair and courteous in your arguments. Never get involved in a quarrel or become angry, regardless of what is said. Let us speak about our faith in all wisdom, redeeming the time. Speak with grace and never demean the person to whom you are witnessing *(Colossians 4.2-6)*.

4. Always be ready to give your testimony
(Romans 10.9-10; 1 Peter 3.15)

We must always be intentional about witnessing to others. Begin conversation with them as you would with any other person. Share your own testimony of conversion. This is something every Christian should be able to do without being an experienced theologian or preacher. Explain and express the assurance we have about Heaven and the protection of the Lord. Never underestimate the power of a personal testimony. God invites all men, including Muslims, to call upon Him, with the promise: 'Call unto me, and I will answer thee, and shew thee great and mighty things, which thou knowest not' *(Jeremiah 33.3)*. Muslims like to hear about the transforming power of God in the life of a person. Give some examples of how God has answered your prayers. Let them know how to find peace with God *(Isaiah 26.3; John 14.27; Romans 5.1; Colossians 1.20)*. In giving your testimony, make it simple and do not exaggerate in the telling.

I know of an Egyptian, who when converted, was wondering how he could witness to his wife. By the grace of the Lord Jesus he completely changed his way of thinking and how he related to her. In his becoming a new creature in Christ his wife was amazed by his new conduct and life, service and love. When she asked him to account for this great change, he told her that it was because of a new Friend Who now gave him good advice. She insisted on knowing about the Friend; and this was how he could then speak to her about the Lord Jesus Christ. Later, she too found the Lord. So we point men and women to the Lord Jesus Christ.

5. Avoid stereotypes or generalisations

See people clearly without prejudice. We should not assume that Muslims are not interested in the Gospel or that they don't want to hear anything about it. Not every Muslim is an extremist, an Arab or a Sheik, or intolerant or a polygamist. Let the Muslim understand that there is a difference between Christianity and the Western ethos, for stereotypes work both ways. 'Muslim' is a religious term. A Muslim is someone who adheres to the religion of Islam. 'Arab', on the other hand, is an ethno-linguistic term; and Arabs speak the Arabic language. It is true that Islam originated among the Arabs, and that the Qur'an was written in Arabic, but not all Muslims are Arabs (eg: the Turks, the Kurds, the Iranians, the Pakistanis, the Malaysians, the Indonesians, and several nations in Africa), and not all Arabs are Muslims.

6. Use the Word of God

Don't give the impression that you believe that the Qur'an is a book revealed by God. Read from the Bible; do not just quote it. We want people to hear the Gospel, so only refer to the Qur'an if really necessary. Urge the inquirer to read the Bible (especially the New Testament) without prejudice. Most Muslims who have found the Lord have been converted, not by the power of argument, but by reading the Bible. It is always better to invite a Muslim inquirer to purchase a Bible, as a person is seldom appreciative of what he gets free. Do not give Bibles away unwisely and without discernment. To the Muslim mind, if the Bible is so precious, it must cost something. It is better when someone asks for it, and far better when someone buys it. That way it will be valued. We can, of course, give them the New Testament, and portions of the Scriptures.

Do not use a torn or defaced Bible. We have already observed how

Muslims like to see that we show respect to our Holy Book. Do not put it on the floor or casually cast it on the table after using it, or they will be offended and not listen to you. Avoid using a red letter Bible with Muslims, or they will think only the words in red are from God and the others are not. (And a Bible should certainly never be taken to the bathroom or lavatory, let alone left there.)

The *Gospel of Matthew* is the best known among Muslim scholars because it contains the Beatitudes and the whole Sermon on the Mount. Suggest the *Gospel of Matthew* for a starting place.

7. Ask thought-provoking questions

Questions help to avoid any ambiguity and lead straight to the point. For example: Do you know where you will spend life after death? Who is God? Why would a holy God let *you* into Heaven? What do you understand by the assertion that Jesus Christ is the Son of God? Can you know for sure if you are saved or not? Are your sins forgiven? Do you have an answer for why there is suffering in the world? Why can't a person live a holy life? Why is sin in the world? May I show you what the Bible teaches? Have you heard about the real Lord Jesus? Have you ever read the Bible?

Ask people what they understand about the creation, the Fall, and sin. Do they know that one sin is enough to send a sinner to hell? Do they understand why there is death and suffering?

As Christians we should ensure that we can explain these things to Muslims. The Bible has all the answers. Show how sin pollutes all human beings, and the need we therefore have of a Saviour. Show the inquirer that you regard Heaven, hell, sin, and spiritual things as matters of life and death. Muslims believe that Allah, being omnipotent, can do anything, even simply 'overlook' and 'forgive' sin without requiring punishment. Tell them that the God of the Bible is holy, and explain what God's holiness actually means – He must punish sin – either in the sinner or in a substitute, His own Son.

In speaking about Christ, always use one of His titles or offices:

Jesus Christ, the Lord Jesus, Jesus the Saviour or the Redeemer, etc. It shows respect to Him. They do the same to every prophet they name. If you pray in their presence, close your prayer with the same respectful titles or offices, not a hurried, 'In the name of Jesus.' He is God, after all.

- Explain to Muslims that we do not believe in or worship three gods, but one God in three Persons.
- Help them see that to believe in Christ is not *Shirk* (apostasy), and that Christ is entirely what and who He says He is *(Surah 3.48)*. Actually in their case they have elevated Muhammad to the level of deity.
- Tell them that salvation is only by grace through faith *(Ephesians 2.8-10)*. Explain what 'grace' is and what 'faith' means.
- Point out the importance of repentance of sin. Christianity is the faith of the broken and contrite heart *(Psalm 51.17)*, not of spiritual complacency or spiritual pride generated by self-righteousness.

8. Do not engage in useless polemics or debates

Avoid confrontational discussions. Be ready to listen and do not rush to answer, but politely ensure you are also listened to *(James 1.19; cf. Proverbs 15.28; 18.13; 29.20)*. Do not be drawn into games of tit-for-tat; always be prepared to answer wisely and with meekness *(1 Peter 3.15)*. To repeat what we have already said, your aim is not to win the argument, or gain points in an awkward debate; it is by God's grace that souls are won for Christ. Keep focused, and do not get distracted or carried away. Instead of arguing, explain the biblical concept of God's love, holiness, forgiveness, hope and salvation. Avoid the vicious circle of questions. Remember that the Bible and the Gospel are self-authenticating. As Spurgeon said, the Bible can take care of itself. As we speak, we must also aim to remove misconceptions which hinder the Gospel message. Tact and discretion are needed. Though there will be disagreement, we must show honour and respect.

9. Use one-to-one interaction

Family bonds are everything to Muslims. They live as a community (generally speaking). They belong to one another. There is no individual, there is only community. Each one is afraid that his friend will report his interest in the Gospel to the local imam, or to his parents and relatives. So they will feel a need to defend Islam in the presence of other Muslims, especially in the West. Individual contact is always the best way, because people are often sensitive to pressure or to the possibility of losing face ('losing face' is far more important in the East than in the West). The ideal is for men to speak with men and women to speak with women, because Islamic societies often impose restrictions on contact between unmarried men and women. Failure to respect such rules will badly hurt our witness. It is good to bear in mind that Muslim women (even in the West) are not used to making decisions, because their fathers or even brothers normally decide for them. Some women will not shake hands with men (let them initiate it; if not, refrain). Remember that many Muslims regards all Westerners as immoral and decadent.

Do not feel that they will be offended if you invite them for dinner. For a meal, please serve *Halal* food, for the kingdom of God is not about food and drink *(Romans 14.17; 1 Corinthians 8.8)*. Do not hand anything to them with your left hand (which is considered unclean). Pork is forbidden, and to offer it will cause huge offence. If you have a pet dog, keep it out of the way where possible, and certainly don't pat it in front of a Muslim, as it is considered to be 'unclean'. Likewise, do not be surprised when your guest is not impressed by the welcoming mood of your dog!

We should do in our homes as Mary and Martha did and have a warm welcome ready *(Luke 10.38-42)*. Home is the perfect place for expressing and explaining our faith to Muslims. There is no law against hospitality and friendship, and these qualities are highly valued right across the Muslim world. In many cases, hospitality is the door to their hearts.

Never neglect to say grace, especially when they are your guests. Visit them in their home, and don't wait to be invited. Your unsolicited visit will be seen as a pleasant surprise and as a sign of friendship. You can honour a Muslim by visiting him. Remember time is not so important for the average Muslim. The fasting month of Ramadan is not an ideal time for door to door visitation. If you are a man, never visit your Muslim neighbour if only women are at home. Adopt a conservative and modest dress code.

Limit the spiritual discussion to one or two subjects: by doing so you place limits on the conversation and avoid jumping from one subject to another. The discussion should always lead to a definite conclusion. Keep your goal steadily in mind. Where necessary explain any theological terms used – such as the new birth, salvation, the blood of Christ, expiation, Son of God, atonement, the Holy Spirit, the Gospel, etc.

Contrary to what most books on how to reach Muslims teach, don't avoid the terms 'Son of God' or 'Trinity'. Explain these terms with simple words, because they are misunderstood by Muslims. Make it clear that we don't believe that Mary is the 'wife' of God, or that the Lord Jesus is the Son of God in a physical sense.

Speak about Christ's miraculous and sinless life, the many prophecies about Him; the meanings of His names; where He is now, and His return which will bring a close to this world.

10. Pray and persevere

(Ephesians 6.18; Colossians 4.2-3; 1 Thessalonians 5.17)

As it is often said, prayer changes things. We are involved in a spiritual battle; prayer and intercession are of paramount importance. Our weapons are spiritual, not carnal *(2 Corinthians 10.3-5)*. Take the initiative to reach out in compassion to every sinner in a humble spirit. We must earnestly ask the Holy Spirit to guide us. Be patient in witnessing to the same people more than once. We prayerfully depend upon the Lord for every opportunity. Pray for an open door. Be wise as a serpent and harmless as a dove *(Matthew 10.16)*. Use every opportunity to witness wisely and gently, in season and out of season *(2 Timothy 4.2)*. As with most sinners, Muslims need to hear the Gospel more than once before it is understood, and before the Holy Spirit brings them to a deep conviction of sin and their need of the Saviour. Endeavour to learn *when* to speak and *how much* to say. Be humble and speak kindly. 'A soft answer turneth away wrath: but grievous words stir up anger' *(Proverbs 15.1)*. Let them see and know that we pray (not ritually), and that we also pray for them.

We cannot overstate the importance of prayer and of a regular prayer life to strengthen our witness. Pray that others may receive the gift of eye and heart-opening *(Acts 16.14)*. More is wrought by patient, persevering prayer than we dare hope. Muslims are usually very patient; and so we must be also. You can at least encourage yourself that you are reaching someone who believes in God, not a cold and resistant atheist.

11. Never say anything negative about the Qur'an, Muhammad and Muslims

We do not want to embarrass or upset Muslims. We should not criticise their religion. Do not debate or question Muhammad as a prophet, and do not talk about his many wives or about his cruelty or life. That is not profitable, and if you attack his person or his morality you will inevitably inflame passions and 'lose' your hearer. Do not enter into political discussions. Avoid controversial secular matters (such as Palestine and Israel), and all trivial matters. Present the facts, the evidence, and the promises in the Bible for all who put their trust in the Lord Jesus. Present the evidence which shows the Bible is true and has never suffered any corruption.

12. Do not anticipate instant conversions

Conversions are the work of the Holy Spirit, even though we believe in human instrumentality. We do not expect to both sow and reap the same day. Evangelism requires prayer, patience and perseverance. It is a marathon race rather than a sprint. In the case where a Muslim is genuinely seeking, we should not pressurise him to make a 'decision' for Christ. Allow him to become a Christian, not a 'Westerner'.

A Muslim must know there is a price to pay when he leaves Islam, for even though salvation is by grace, he should never think grace is without consequences. When a Muslim has sought and found the Lord, allow the convert – not you – to openly confess it. Do not propel him to the forefront as if he were a trophy to put on display.

13. Our confession and our five pillars

Against the five pillars advocated by Muslims, Christians can speak about their five pillars or the 'Five Solas' of Reformation truth (and also the five doctrines of grace).

– **Sola Scriptura or by Scripture alone:** The Holy Bible (containing the Old and New Testaments) is entirely inspired by God as the all-sufficient, final authority in all matters of faith and practice. The Bible is truthful and reliable, and above traditions and the opinions of men.

– **Sola Fide or by faith alone:** Justification before God is by faith alone 'without the deeds of the law' *(Romans 3.28)*; 'without faith it is impossible to please [God]...' *(Hebrews 11.6)*.

– **Sola Gratia or by grace alone:** Grace is God's unmerited free gift and favour. Salvation is solely by grace through faith *(Ephesians 2.8-10)*. We do not contribute anything to it. All that we have is by grace *(2 Timothy 1.9)*.

– **Solus Christus or by Christ alone:** Christ is the only and sufficient Mediator between God and men. His work on the cross of Calvary is fully sufficient to purchase salvation for His people.

– **Soli Deo Gloria or glory to God alone:** The ultimate purpose of salvation is to bring glory and praise to God the Father through the Lord Jesus Christ by the power of the Holy Spirit.

A word of conclusion

'The whole world lieth in wickedness' *(1 John 5.19).* Islam denies great foundational doctrines of paramount importance for Christians and for the salvation of humanity. It controverts the deity and the sonship of Christ. It contradicts His death, His substitutionary atonement, and His resurrection. In most Islamic nations, Christians have no right to exist. In others, they are only tolerated. Exclusion and persecution are already in so many lands around the globe. Some Islamic countries are determined to eradicate Christianity completely.

Unfortunately many Muslims have never been introduced to true Christianity, and sadly most of them have never met a true Christian, and have never heard the true Gospel. They do not know the Lord, and we should not assume that they know the Bible or understand true Christianity.

If everyone who claimed to be a Christian were a genuine Christian, Islam would have collapsed a long time ago. Uncommitted, unbalanced and compromising Christians have caused enormous damage to the faith, and have set themselves up as an easy target for Muslims to proselytise. Churches must preach about true repentance, and avoid shallow conversions where no change takes place in the life of the sinner. Islam, as with other religions and atheism, is the inevitable consequence of God giving us up to our sins. We must pray that the 'scales' will fall from their eyes, and that the light of the glorious Gospel of Christ, Who is the image of God, will shine upon them. We must pray that God will be pleased to use us as instruments in the harvest of Muslim souls. May He give us the needed passion!

'The fruit of the righteous is a tree of life;
and he that winneth souls is wise' *(Proverbs 11.30).*